W9-CAP-531

PHILOSOPHY
IN THE
MODERN AGE

PHIL 203

Mount St. Mary's University

Copyright © 2016 by Mount St. Mary's University.
All rights reserved
Printed in the United States of America

ISBN 13: 978-1-50669-619-5

No part of this book may be reproduced in any manner without permission in writing from the publisher.

Cover photo: © Mount St. Mary's University

Acknowledgment:

pp. 1–18: from *Souls in Transition: The Religious and Spiritual Lives of Emerging Adults* by Christian Smith. Copyright © 2009 by Oxford University Press. Reprinted by permission of the publisher via the Copyright Clearance Center.

530 Great Road
Acton, MA 01720
800-562-2147
www.xanedu.com

Contents

PHILOSOPHY IN THE MODERN AGE

PHIL 203

from Souls in Transition

Christian Smith

It is crucial to understand the religious and spiritual worlds of emerging adults within the broader context of the larger cultural worlds in which they live and which they use to construct their own lives. Emerging adults' religious and spiritual assumptions, experiences, outlooks, beliefs, and practices do not exist in compartmentalized isolation from their larger cultural worldviews and lived experiences but are often related to and powerfully shaped by them. Before launching into our analysis of emerging adults' religious and spiritual lives, therefore, we need to provide an orienting overview of these larger cultural worlds. We will describe a number of prevailing, mainstream themes that emerged from the 230 personal interviews. Interspersed among these main themes we mention some less commonly voiced ones that indicate differing cultural emphases among smaller numbers of emerging adults, providing a counterpoint to the most common ones.

It is impossible to convey in one summarizing chapter like this the full richness and complexity of contemporary emerging adult culture. We are talking about 46 million young people in the United States whose lives encompass personal outlooks and experiences as diverse as those seen in the previous chapter. Most of today's emerging adults do share many elements of a common culture, which we seek to describe here. But even within that common culture we find different emphases, experiences, and cultural expressions. This summary chapter therefore unavoidably over-simplifies the actual reality of emerging adult culture, even as it works to provide some balance and complexity in the process.

• • •

Hard to See an Objective Reality Beyond the Self

The majority of emerging adults can express very well how people are shaped and bound by their personal subjective experiences. But most have great difficulty grasping the idea that a reality that is objective to their own awareness or construction of it may exist that could have a significant bearing on their lives. In philosophical terms, most emerging adults functionally (meaning how they actually think and act, regardless of the theories they hold) are soft ontological antirealists and epistemological skeptics and perspectivalists—although few have any conscious idea what those terms mean. They seem to presuppose that they are simply imprisoned in their own subjective selves, limited to their biased interpretations of their own sense perceptions, unable to know the real truth of anything beyond themselves. They are de facto doubtful that an identifiable, objective, shared reality might exist across and around all people that can serve as a reliable reference point for rational deliberation and argument. So, for example, when we interviewers tried to get respondents to talk about whether what they take to be substantive moral beliefs reflect some objective or universal quality or standard are simply relative human inventions, many—if not most—could not understand what we interviewers were trying to get at. They had difficulty seeing the possible distinction between, in this case, objective moral truth and relative human invention. This is not because they are dumb. It seems to be because they simply cannot, for whatever reason, believe in—or sometimes even conceive of—a given, objective truth, fact, reality, or nature of the world that is independent of their subjective self-experience and that in relation to which they and others might learn or be persuaded to change. Although none would put it in exactly this way, what emerging adults take to be reality ultimately seems to consist of a multitude of subjective but ultimately autonomous experiences. People are thus trying to communicate with each other in order to simply be able to get along and enjoy life as they see fit. Beyond that, anything truly objectively shared or common or real seems impossible to access.

• • •

Right and Wrong Are Easy

When asked how difficult or easy it is to know right and wrong in life today, nearly all respondents said it is easy. Many hardly had to even think about it. When then asked how hard it is to know right and wrong—regardless of how difficult it is to do what is morally right—again, nearly everyone said it is easy. Morality is like common sense; unless you are actively resisting it, it is not hard to know what to do or to do it. The vast majority are moral intuitionists—that is, they believe that they know what is right and wrong by attending to the subjective feelings or intuitions that they sense within themselves when they find themselves in various situations or facing ethical questions. Those subjective moral intuitions are themselves reported to be the product of right moral principles implanted deeply within their consciences when they were children by their parents, teachers, pastors, and other adult authorities. That early moral socialization, their implicit account goes, is ineradicable and reliable. Having been laid down early and deep, the moral principles cannot be removed or altered. All one has to do is pay some attention to what one feels or intuits in any situation and one will definitely know what is the morally right thing to do. In this way, emerging adults profess to be navigating the moral challenges of life with relative proficiency and ease. Some say that their deeply ingrained moral principles guide them to form their relationships and practices in such ways that they actually rarely even have to face a difficult moral problem or choice in the first place. Moral difficulties are simply precluded and averted by structuring life in ways that avoid them to begin with. The majority of emerging adults interviewed had difficulty thinking of even one example of a situation recently when they had some trouble deciding what was the morally right or wrong thing to do. Most of those who finally did come up with an example pointed to the moral and emotional difficulty they had in deciding whether or not to break up with a boyfriend or girlfriend. In short, thinking and living morally is quite effortless—you merely pay attention to your inner self, and it all comes fairly naturally. So in discussions about knowing right from wrong and doing the right thing, they almost uniformly offered the following kinds of replies. "I base a lot off instincts, I was brought up with a good idea of what was right and wrong, and if it was okay my head and heart tell me. I don't think it's very hard." "It's pretty easy, I just stay away from certain situations. That hasn't really changed, it's just easy for me." "Usually it's not hard, usually the wrong choice kinda glares at me like, 'No! Wrong!'" "Doing the right thing, it's pretty easy. I would feel bad if I knew it was wrong." "I've always been a really quick decision-maker. Making decisions has never been hard for me, so in terms of wrong and right, it kinda clicks in my head." "Intuition, sort of. I use judgment with everything like, it just kinda comes naturally. I can't think of anything that really actively influences me to decide what's right or wrong, or good or bad. Maybe it's just sort of how I've developed as a person that kinda helps things like that along." "I know in my heart if it's something that I'm just not comfortable doing, I would feel uncomfortable doing in my heart. I would say it's pretty easy to know. I have kind of a gut feeling with some things, so overall, it's pretty easy to trust my own instincts."

Not Hurting Others Is Self-Evident

One of the core principles emerging adults seem to presuppose in thinking about moral behavior is the imperative not to hurt others. "Others" here means anyone else. In this, they are essentially ethical consequentialists: if something would hurt another person, it is probably bad; if it does not and is not illegal, it's probably fine. Curiously, very few emerging adults—probably like many adults as well—are able to explain exactly why they think hurting others is morally wrong. To them it is just obvious. As interviewers, we pointed out that more than a few people and tribes and cultures in history and around the world have not thought hurting others outside of their in-groups to be particularly bad. Some people positively enjoy hurting others. But that information did not change respondents' thinking, nor did it seem to prod them to try to better explain why hurting others is a categorical wrong. They did not appeal, for instance, to God's will, natural law, utilitarian principles, the Bible, or any other supposed source of universal moral truth to justify this belief. "Don't hurt others" functions instead as a kind of free-floating, unjustified supposition that informs intuitive moral feelings and opinions. Sometimes respondents might say that hurting another person would make them feel bad about themselves or that they would not want to live in a society in which everyone hurt everyone else. But why that itself should count in a moral argument they cannot say. In the end, they have difficulty explaining why the thinking of someone else who does not believe hurting others is wrong is in fact incorrect.

Karma Will Catch You

A surprising number of those interviewed—not a majority, but more than a few—spontaneously, explicitly referred to "karma" as a way to explain why it's best to act morally and why the universe is ultimately a just place. In evoking karma, they meant that good attitudes and behavior will be rewarded in this life and bad will get what it deserves, too. "What goes around comes around," they explained. "Karma's a bitch," another said, making the point that you can't escape its merciless consequences. Talking about karma does not mean these emerging adults have any real interest in or knowledge about Hinduism, Sikhism, or Buddhism or believe in reincarnation. Nor was it merely a hip shorthand for describing societal social control or divine judgment. Many did not even seem aware of those possible connections. Rather, karma appears to have become a shared, pop culture way of explaining the fair operations of good and bad in the world—among emerging adults, at least. Karma functions as a reminder for emerging adults that they can't get away with bad stuff. It catches up to you. It pays off in the future to do the right thing. Bad people will get theirs. Almost everyone basically gets what he or she deserves. Karma helps keep some moral justice in the world. At the same time, karma does not require belief in a specific God or commitment to a particular religious tradition. Karma does not necessitate involvement in a religious congregation or the exercise of any particular spiritual or religious self-disciplines. Nor does karma specify any long-term—particularly afterlife—consequences for living different sorts of moral lives. Karma is much more palatable and individually manageable than, say, belief in a final judgment, divine rewards and punishments, and especially heaven and hell. In short, while nobody can escape karma, neither does karma displace the final authority of individuals over their own lives.

Everybody's Different

If people in the world represent complex combinations of similarities and differences, emerging adults in the United States today tend mostly to see the differences. Conversations with them clearly reveal their great sensitivity to the belief "Everybody's different," as they frequently say. Nearly any question asked of them about any norm, experience, rule of thumb, expectation, or belief in life is very likely to get an answer beginning with the phrase "Well, everybody's different, but for me . . . " Although nobody expresses the underlying viewpoint in so many words, it seems to be that humans share very little in common with each other, that you can't count on any common features or interests across people that binds them together or gives them a basis on which to work out disagreements. And the differences emphasized are not merely cross-cultural dissimilarities between, say, Americans and Chinese. As in well-known postmodernist theory, the differences actually drive down to individual personalities. Any given person has his or her own unique beliefs, tastes, feelings, thoughts, desires, and expectations. Nobody can presume to impose on or perhaps even fully understand those of another. Literally every individual is different. This, it seems, is not merely basic American individualism. It is individualism raised on heavy doses of multiculturalism and pumped up on the steroids of the postmodern insistence on disjuncture, *differance*, and differences "going all the way down." Few emerging adults have actually read Jacques Derrida or Stanley Fish, but their effects seem to have trickled down in this way into popular prereflective consciousness among this population nonetheless. And so interviewers heard them saying things like "I think the last few years have made me more aware of [how] what's right for me may be wrong for someone else or what's wrong for me may be okay for somebody else. I think it's made me more aware of other people's feelings about things." Concerning religious faith, one said, "You know, the Muslim religion is not right for me, but it doesn't make it wrong for them. I just think it's all subjective to each person. I really do think that everything is pretty much subjective." And to the question about how much material stuff people should buy and own or not own, another replied, "That's a personal choice. I don't know, I guess that's personal for everybody."

It's Up to the Individual

It is hardly surprising, in light of much of the foregoing, that according to emerging adults, the absolute authority for every person's beliefs or actions is his or her own sovereign self. Anybody can literally think or do whatever he or she wants. Of course, what a person chooses to think or do may have bad consequences for that person. But everything is ultimately up to each individual to decide for himself or herself. The most one should ever do toward influencing another person is to ask him or her to consider what one thinks. Nobody is bound to any course of action by virtue of belonging to a group or because of a common good. Individuals are autonomous agents who have to deal with each other, yes; but do so entirely as self-directing choosers. The words *duty, responsibility,* and *obligation* feel somehow vaguely coercive or puritanical. Saying that somebody "should" do something is about as far as many emerging adults are comfortable going. You can't make anybody do anything, so don't even try to influence them. Stick to what you think is right. Tell others what you think, if they ask you. But respect the fact that everything is finally the other's own call. Thus, one respondent explained, "I have no other way of knowing what to do morally but how I internally feel. That's where my decisions come from. From me, from inside of me." Another said about the source of her own moral beliefs: "I think mostly myself. Some from religion, I guess, some from parents. But, I think for me to actually pick my views, I mean, it has to come from me." When asked what it is that makes anything right or wrong, another replied, "I think it's your own personal belief system. I don't think it's anything like social norms or like that. I think it's just what you think, it's dependent on each person and their own beliefs and what they think is right or wrong." Thus, as applied to the issue of people having any responsibilities related to material wealth and possessions, for instance, another said, "If someone works for their three billion dollars that they own, it's rightfully their three billion dollars. They should be able to buy whatever they want. Yeah, I think they should at least help some people out, but it's their money, they can do what they want. If they want to go out and get 40 different cars, whatever, that is [fine]."

More Open-Minded

Emerging adults, when reflecting on how they have changed since high school, often say that they have "become more open-minded" or "accepting of different ideas or lifestyles." They seem to mean this in a variety of senses. Generally, they explain that when they were younger they tended to embrace fairly rigidly the views they were raised to hold. Since high school, however, they report having been exposed to a greater variety of kinds of people and lifestyles and viewpoints, to which they have often tried to be open and work out accommodating responses. For some this means dropping old prejudices or fears. For others this means loosening up the boundaries of their moral views or beliefs about what is safe or wise. Some have become "more open-minded" by starting to drink alcohol when their parents raised them to be against drinking. Some mean that they used to think that something was wrong with gays and lesbians but they've since come to believe that they are perfectly normal, or at least that it is misguided to try to oppose them. Others have become much more sexually active since high school, which they view as becoming more liberal or open-minded. Often, shifts in these directions do not signify major lifestyle or value transformations but rather marginal or incremental shifts toward freedom and acceptance, compared to somewhat more restrictive beliefs held in high school or to parents' current views. One emerging adult, for example, said,

> I have quite transitioned. I went from a sweet little innocent kid that perhaps had some morals left, to a dirty hippy with none. I have morals, but yeah, so, it's been good. [So what's the transition been about?] Nothing in particular, just I guess getting older, going to college, just meeting new people, and I'm just, I don't know, not exactly a new outlook on life, just a new like, I'm a little more casual about everything now. So I don't, I'm not so, like, uptight about everything as I used to be.

All Cultures Are Relative

Related to the previous point, when it comes to culture, most emerging adults seem to be what sociologists call social constructionists, whether they know it or not. That is, they mostly unquestioningly presuppose that most things about the sociocultural world are not fixed or given facts of nature but rather human constructions invented through shared social definitions and practices that are historically contingent, changeable, and particular. It apparently has not required the taking of multiple anthropology, sociology, and postmodern humanities classes for most emerging adults to have arrived at this view. For many, it appears that the sheer impact of the simple realization of the particularity of the conditions in which they were raised drives them to assume this de facto social constructionism. "When they were younger, as for everybody, their personally experienced reality was, for them, simply reality. Now that they have grown older, have met some different people, and maybe have seen some of the world, they seem keenly aware that they were raised in a very particular way that is different from the way others were raised. Sociology and anthropology show that human cultures are indeed significantly socially constructed and vary in certain ways across time and space. That awareness by most emerging adults presses them—for better or worse—to relativize their own perspectives. For instance, they repeatedly frame and qualify their views on life with statements such as "Well, at least for how I was raised I feel that . . ." and "For other people it's different, but for me I tend to think that . . ." For example, one respondent observed, "Being raised in a certain culture you have certain norms for what are moral, I guess for me there is certain way to act based on my culture. But if someone else is coming with a different perspective, they would maybe have a different outcome, based on what they believe." Often these are not intentionally expressed statements of feelings-replacing-thought or opinions-replacing-beliefs, but rather unconscious habits of speech reflecting larger cultural norms. To whatever degree it is intentional, however, the phrase "I feel that" has nearly ubiquitously replaced the phrases "I think that," "I believe that," and "I would argue that"—a shift in language use that expresses an essentially subjectivistic and emotivistic approach to moral reasoning and rational argument. Consider, for instance, this emerging adult's use of "feel" 12 times in seven sentences:

> Morality is how I feel too, because in my heart, I could feel it. You could feel what's right or wrong in your heart as well as your mind.

> Most of the time, I always felt, I feel it in my heart, and it makes it easier for me to morally decide what's right and wrong. Because if I feel about doing something, I'm going to feel it in my heart. And if it feels good, then I'm going to do it. But if it doesn't feel good, I'm going to know. Because then I'm going to be nervous, and I'm going to be tensed, and it's not going to feel good. It's not going to feel right. So it's like I got that feeling as well as thinking.

One of the apparent effects of this culturally relativistic view and the continual self-relativizing to which it leads is speech in which claims are not staked, rational arguments are not developed, differences are not engaged, nature (as in the natural world, the reality beyond what humans make up) is not referenced, and universals are not recognized. Rather, differences in viewpoints and ways of life are mostly acknowledged, respected, and then set aside as incommensurate and off limits for evaluation.

Relative Morality Depends on the Case

Following from the previous two themes, most emerging adults view morality as ultimately a personal, relative affair: morally right and wrong beliefs depend entirely on the specifics of the case and the "opinions" of the people involved. Not many grasp a strong sense of a natural or universal moral standard or law that in any way transcends human invention. To be sure, most emerging adults seem to believe in moral right and wrong. But when they are pressed, it becomes clear that for them, the moral character of a matter is ultimately rooted in the beliefs, socialization, and feelings of the individuals involved. In philosophical language—in which few have any formal training—most emerging adults seem to be believers in simplified versions of G. E. Moore's antinaturalistic moral emotivism and Richard Rorty's relativistic moral pragmatism. Again, it is difficult for emerging adults—lacking access or appeal to any real moral reference point independent of their own subjective perceptions, socialization, and experience—to see how commonly binding moral judgments might be rationally justified or moral disagreements adjudicated. All that humans finally have, they assume, is each person's experience, and different people see things different ways, so the best that anyone can do is to obey civil laws and not hurt each other. (Exactly what moral principles deserve to be institutionalized in law and why is often an opaque matter beyond their ability to explain; but in true pragmatic fashion, figuring that out actually doesn't often matter as much, for many, as simply knowing what in fact is in the law and working with it.) In the end, few emerging adults are equipped to make and explain broadly applicable, reasoned moral judgments. What they do instead is either form their own strong "opinions" and keep them to themselves or dismiss such concerns as impossible and simply do their best to live up to the beliefs they learned as they were raised. Case in point: In the middle of explaining that for religious reasons she does not believe in cohabitation before marriage, a young evangelical woman, who is devoted to gospel missionary work overseas, interrupted herself with this observation: "I don't know. I think everyone is different so, I know it wouldn't work for me, but it could work for someone else."

A Less Typical Theme—Rights and Wrongs are Objectively Real.

We said earlier that most emerging adults in the United States have difficulty conceiving of a reliable, objective reality beyond individual selves in relation to which one might make reasoned evaluations of the worth of the self's beliefs, feelings, and desires—whether one's own or others'. We also said that most of them embrace the kind of cultural and moral relativism produced by a vulgar social constructionism, and that morality and ethics are viewed in highly personal and situational terms. This is the mainstream view among emerging adults. But an alternative minority view runs counter to the majority. According to some, certain definite things are good and bad, right and wrong, just and unjust, and that human beings as such can and should know them and live accordingly. This minority is unconvinced by arguments about cultural difference and relativism. Everything is not relative. There are clear moral rights and wrongs, even if some people want to pretend otherwise. These emerging adults believe they know—whether through common sense, the nature of universal reality, or divine revelation—that truth and goodness exist and that people can learn these and be responsible for them. Like Amanda, when they hear of peers expressing relativistic ideas, they dismiss it as self-indulgent rationalizing of wrong choices and behaviors for which their peers do not want to be held responsible. They themselves seek to live morally, with more integrity according to what they know is good, true, and right. One respondent, for example, reasoned: "Are we going to get to a point that culture's going to evolve so much that the principle of not murdering is obsolete? No! That's wrong, you know? Or maybe there are certain circumstances that are very special, very narrow, very rare sort of circumstances. But I don't care if it's a thousand years down the road, how far we are from biblical times, murder is never going to be okay." Another argued: "I think there are definitely some issues that I don't find those to be gray areas. I think some issues are wrong and some issues are right."

Uncertain Purpose

Some emerging adults have settled on what seems to be a clear and strong sense of purpose in life. But they are the minority. At ages 18 to 23, most are still sorting out what their purpose in life might be, to what good they want to devote themselves. Here we mean not mainly some philosophical "ultimate purpose of life"—what the Germans call "God-and-the-world" questions—but rather the more prosaic issue of what one as a person ought to be doing with one's life. Nearly all emerging adults have a general vision, as we will show, of what a "good life" looks like. But more specific questions about careers and causes and life devotions are as yet unformed. Some are impatient about spending time in this limbo; others are relaxed and patient, trying to enjoy the freedoms and pleasures of young life while they last. But either way, this position certainly and inescapably involves uncertainty—a general lack of sureness, direction, and intention. It sounds like this: "I feel like I should have more done with my life right now, but also, like people my age, don't have it all figured out like they used to. So I'm not really sure what to think, I guess, about my own goals, and I'll do what I can do." And this:

> I would say it's still a little unclear about my purpose. I don't know what I want to be when I grow up. I know it's a little late for that, but I still don't know what I want to be. I know that for right now what I'm going to do is just keep doing what I'm doing until it comes to me. I guess as far as the bigger picture purpose, I don't know what there is for me yet. But I'm not worried about it either.

And like this:

I've noticed a lot of people really upset and stressed not knowing what they want to do with their life. I know so many people that just get, like, broken down because they just have no idea what they wanna do, where they wanna go. Some people are dropping out of school because they need to do some self-exploration before they're sure that they wanna go to this institution that costs so much. Some of my friends are dropping out of college just because it's so expensive, and they don't know what they wanna do anymore. So they don't feel it's worth it. For a lot of people it's really kind of earth-shattering because things that they thought they wanted to do their entire life, they suddenly realize they don't. So right now, the biggest challenge for most people my age, is the transition from being a kid, like, from high school when you're like, "Yeah, future looks great," to starting to transition into the real world, I mean it's still college and a lot of people are like "best time of your life," sorta like a dream world, no responsibility. But everything's kinda looming on the horizon right now. That's a big challenge.

Education Is of Instrumental Value

Many, though not all, emerging adults believe in the importance of finishing high school and getting a college education. Large numbers want to go to university, do well in school, get a degree, and put it to use. But for most, the motivating reasons behind their valuing higher education seem to have almost entirely to do with the instrumental advantages it produces—as well as the fun one can have while in college. "What matters is getting the credits, earning the diploma, and becoming certified as a college-educated person so that one can get a better job, earn more money, and become a good salary earner and supporter of a (materially) comfortable and secure life. Not very many emerging adults talk about the intrinsic value of an education, of the personal broadening and deepening of one's understanding and appreciation of life and the world that expansive learning affords. Few talk about the value of a broad education for shaping people into informed and responsible citizens in civic life, for producing leaders and members who can work together toward the common good of all in society. An articulation of an understanding of the enduring worth of a broad liberal arts education for the development of persons and the sustaining of humanistic societies is not often heard from this age group. For most, higher education is good instead because—besides the fun one can have while in college—it promises to help secure for individuals more rewarding jobs, higher income, and so greater personal prospects for material and psychological well-being and security. For some, that means really learning information and skills. For example, one respondent said, "Right now I'm studying marketing, but I think I am going to change it to finance and accounting, so anything in business really. Because business is a very solid thing. Businesses are going to be around for a long time. There will always be jobs, and I like math, so, accounting." For others, higher education is just so many hoops to have to jump through, whether in classrooms or over the Internet. Another respondent, for instance, said:

> Once I did find a job [I realized] it would be so much easier to do well if I did have a degree, just because of the way access is given people. People just recognize you more if you have a degree. That's why I decided to go back to school. But, really my heart is in the work that I do. If I didn't need to be in school, I wouldn't.

Either way, those who can afford it are mostly happy to do it because of the instrumental goods it will deliver and fun that college life offers. As one respondent said, "So many people are out of jobs and losing their houses, it's really kinda bad around here, so that's a reason why I want to go to school so I can make sure I get at least a decent job."

• • •

Consumerism Is Good Stuff

The interviews asked a set of questions probing emerging adults' attitudes about materialism and mass-consumerism. We, as the interview guide authors, worked hard to write questions that would not be leading in any way, out of concern that criticizing materialistic consumerism would generate—in today's environmentally conscious culture—social desirability effects, leading respondents to express distress about and condemnation of materialism and shallow consumerism that they really did not in fact feel or believe. As it turned out, that concern was entirely unfounded. Not only was there no danger of

leading emerging adults into expressing false opposition to materialistic consumerism; interviewers could not, not matter how hard they
pushed, get emerging adults to express any serious concerns about any
aspect of mass-consumer materialism. As far as they were concerned—
almost every single emerging adult interviewed—shopping falls on a
spectrum of enjoyment between being simply uninteresting to being
a major source of happiness, and there is little to no problem with the
amount of material stuff everybody owns. As long as people can afford
their purchases, they are fully entitled to buy and consume whatever
they want. There should be no limits to what people might buy and
own, and consuming products is often a great source of satisfaction
that helps to define ultimate goals in life. Voices critical of mass consumerism, materialistic values, or the environmental or social costs of
a consumer-driven economy were nearly nonexistent among emerging
adults. Once the interviewers realized, after a number of interviews,
that they were hardly in danger of leading their respondents into
feigned concern about consumerism, the interviewers began to probe
more persistently to see if there might not be any hot buttons or particular phrases that could tap into any kind of concern about materialistic
consumerism. There were not. Very many of those interviewed simply
could not even understand the issue the interviewers were asking them
about. The idea of having any questions or doubts about the cycle of
shopping, buying, consuming, accumulating, discarding, and shopping appeared to be unthinkable to them. To be sure, an atheist male
who had studied world development in college and described himself
as a socialist said he thought people were too obsessed with what they
could purchase, and perhaps people should limit the material things
they own. But other than him and one or two others, the consensus
position of emerging adults was this: As long as people can afford it,
they may buy and consume whatever they happen to want without
limit. It is completely up to them as individuals. There is nothing at all
problematic about America's consumer-driven socioeconomic system.
Shopping and buying as a way of life is just fine, and owning some of
the nicer things in life is a natural part of the purpose or goal of life.
Here is how it sounded in one conversation:

It feels good to be able to get things that you want, and you worked for the money. If you want something, you go get it. It makes your life become more comfortable, and I guess it just makes you feel good about yourself as well. You want to get something you work for it, and you can get it. [Do you have any particular feelings about all the consumption that Americans do?] I think it's a good thing if you work for it because then you gain that accomplishment and not like you were just given money. "I want to get this, you know, I'll buy that." It's like you actually work for it so you feel that you deserve it, you earned it. You earned that thing that you wanted. You weren't just given it. [Do you think there are limits to what people should possess or own?] I guess everybody has their own needs and wants.

• • •

The Middle-Class Dream Alive and Well

Near the end of the interviews, we interviewers asked emerging adults what they wanted out of life, to describe their life goals and dreams. Nearly all of them replied with some version of the same essential answer: finish education, get a good job, marry, have children, buy a nice house with a yard, raise a family, become financially secure, drive reliable cars, enjoy family vacations, enjoy good relationships, maybe have a dog. In short, nearly all spoke sincerely as if they still-believed in the American middle-class dream and greatly desired to achieve it. Typical was a woman who said, "I really want to have a family and a husband, just, I guess, have that 'American Dream' kind of thing. That's something I've always wanted to do, just after seeing my family and how close they are and how important a husband or a wife is." Respondents voiced very few alternative life dreams, like achieving major social reforms, living overseas, serving the poor, or pursuing any other alternative lifestyles. Not many emerging adults expressed a rabid ambition and materialism that would propel them to seek riches above all else. Many at the lower end of the socioeconomic hierarchy seemed content to achieve a modest version of the middle-class dream—a cozy house, a reasonable income, a decent car—just as long as they could enjoy a close, happy family with those things. Others had larger scale visions than that, describing higher-end lifestyles that they had in mind. But however modest or affluent the dream looked, nearly all described it as attaining material security and happy family life in a comfortable home. One respondent, for instance, said, "Just having a good job, being stable, not having to worry about things, bills and all that, or struggling, being able to pay for the bills, being able to go out once in a while, take a break, just being there with the good things that you want on your own time and just working, having a good job, being able to spend time with family—I think that'll be a good life." Emerging adults' replies to a question they were asked about what they would do with an unexpected inheritance of money, and why, reinforced their answers to the life dream questions. They were asked what they would do with $100,000 if a distant relative died and left it to them. They did not report—as teenagers may more typically say—that they would spend a good chunk of it on nice cars, clothes, travel, and other consumer items. Nearly all said they would invest most or all of it in the stock market, put it in the bank, pay off their credit card loans, finish paying college tuition, use it for the down payment on a house, and similar other, practical, get-a-real-adult-life-started kinds of uses. Some said that when they were younger they would have spent it on cars and fun activities, but now they realize that they have to make provisions for the future. Such fiscal practical-mindedness and investment prudence seems like a new concept to them, but one that is clearly motivated by their drive for financial and family independence and their desire to achieve the middle-class dream of security, comfort, and contentment—described by another as "kind of like the American dream, something you always see and hear about."

Still Believe in America's Freedoms

Interviewers also talked with emerging adults about their view of the United States—about what they see as American society's positive features and strengths, as well as its challenges and problems. They expressed different views on the problems side. But they spoke with near unanimity about America's positives. The best things about America, they said, are its freedoms—of speech, religion, assembly, private property, and so on. Some spoke about American freedom in well-informed and articulate terms, referencing the Bill of Rights, religious plural-ism, and political and civil liberties. Others simply said, "Freedom. Anybody can do whatever they want." But the touchstone of nearly all answers, no matter how elaborate or civically minded, was freedom. America's emerging adults are not, as we will show, very politically interested or involved. But they definitely believe in and appreciate American freedoms, which they view as among the best in the world. Typical was this sentiment! "Of course America has its problems, but I think overall, we are blessed with a lot of freedoms, we have freedom of choice. We can speak our own opinions. Overall we may have our problems as all societies do, but I think it's a good society." Appreciat-ing America's freedom seems closely connected to personal autonomy as a core value of emerging adults. At the same time, we will suggest in this book's conclusion, such a valorizing of personal freedom and autonomy can make it difficult for many emerging adults to "figure out who they really are" and know what a good life—to which it would be worth truly devoting oneself—might look like.

A Less Typical Theme—America Has Major Problems.

Most of the respondents thought that America is not a perfect society but described it as one of the better ones on earth in which to live. They appreciated America's freedoms and valued its material prosper-ity. Often, but not always, they offered various ideas about what prob-lems trouble the United States—such as self-centeredness, poverty, or intolerance. But for the most part, they expressed a benign view of their society and culture. A very small minority dissented from this view-point, however. Some said that America has major problems, without mentioning the positives of freedom. One, for instance, reported, "I feel confident that the United States is in decline from our status of comfort and false securities that we've had about ourselves. I think people are realizing the negative effects of capitalism and are trying to deal with that now and want reparations." Another observed, "It seems that gas prices are getting higher; costs are getting higher, and people are losing jobs, can't find jobs. Maybe it is because I am living on my own now so I see that now, but I see things getting worse."

from The Joyful Wisdom

Friedrich Nietzsche

The Madman

Have you ever heard of the madman who on a bright morning lighted a lantern and ran to the market-place calling out unceasingly: "I seek God! I seek God!"

As there were many people standing about who did not believe in God, he caused a great deal of amusement. Why! is he lost? said one. Has he strayed away like a child? said another. Or does he keep himself hidden? Is he afraid of us? Has he taken a sea-voyage? Has he emigrated?—the people cried out laughingly, all in a hubbub. The insane man jumped into their midst and transfixed them with his glances. "Where is God gone?" he called out.

"I mean to tell you! We have killed him,—you and I! We are all his murderers! But how have we done it? How were we able to drink up the sea? Who gave us the sponge to wipe away the whole horizon? What did we do when we loosened this earth from its sun? Whither does it now move? Whither do we move? Away from all suns? Do we not dash on unceasingly? Backwards, sideways, forewards, in all directions? Is there still an above and below? Do we not stray, as through infinite nothingness? Does not empty space breathe upon us? Has it not become colder? Does not night come on continually, darker and darker? Shall we not have to light lanterns in the morning? Do we not hear the noise of the grave-diggers who are burying God? Do we not smell the divine putrefaction?—for even Gods putrefy! God is dead! God remains dead! And we have killed him!"

"How shall we console ourselves, the most murderous of all murderers? The holiest and the mightiest that the world has hitherto possessed, has bled to death under our knife,—who will wipe the blood from us? With what water could we cleanse ourselves? What lustrums, what sacred games shall we have to devise? Is not the magnitude of this deed too great for us? Shall we not ourselves have to become Gods, merely to seem worthy of it? There never was a greater event,—and on account of it, all who are born after us belong to a higher history than any history hitherto!"

Here the madman was silent and looked again at his hearers; they also were silent and looked at him in surprise. At last he threw his lantern on the ground, so that it broke in pieces and was extinguished. "I come too early," he then said, "I am not yet at the right time. This prodigious event is still on its way, and is travelling,—it has not yet reached men's ears. Lightning and thunder need time, the light of the stars needs time, deeds need time, even after they are done, to be seen and heard. This deed is as yet further from them than the furthest star,—and yet they have done it!"

It is further stated that the madman made his way into different churches on the same day, and there intoned his *Requiem aeternam deo.* When led out and called to account, he always gave the reply: "What are these churches now, if they are not the tombs and monuments of God?"

from Thus Spake Zarathustra

Friedrich Nietzsche

Zarathustra's Prologue

1.

When Zarathustra was thirty years old, he left his home and the lake of his home, and went into the mountains. There he enjoyed his spirit and solitude, and for ten years did not weary of it. But at last his heart changed,—and rising one morning with the rosy dawn, he went before the sun, and spake thus unto it:

Thou great star! What would be thy happiness if thou hadst not those for whom thou shinest!

For ten years hast thou climbed hither unto my cave: thou wouldst have wearied of thy light and of the journey, had it not been for me, mine eagle, and my serpent.

But we awaited thee every morning, took from thee thine overflow and blessed thee for it.

Lo! I am weary of my wisdom, like the bee that hath gathered too much honey; I need hands outstretched to take it.

I would fain bestow and distribute, until the wise have once more become joyous in their folly, and the poor happy in their riches.

Therefore must I descend into the deep: as thou doest in the evening, when thou goest behind the sea, and givest light also to the nether-world, thou exuberant star!

Like thee must I GO DOWN, as men say, to whom I shall descend.

Bless me, then, thou tranquil eye, that canst behold even the greatest happiness without envy!

Bless the cup that is about to overflow, that the water may flow golden out of it, and carry everywhere the reflection of thy bliss!

Lo! This cup is again going to empty itself, and Zarathustra is again going to be a man. Thus began Zarathustra's down-going.

2.

Zarathustra went down the mountain alone, no one meeting him. When he entered the forest, however, there suddenly stood before him an old man, who had left his holy cot to seek roots. And thus spake the old man to Zarathustra:

"No stranger to me is this wanderer: many years ago passed he by. Zarathustra he was called; but he hath altered.

Then thou carriedst thine ashes into the mountains: wilt thou now carry thy fire into the valleys? Fearest thou not the incendiary's doom?

Yea, I recognise Zarathustra. Pure is his eye, and no loathing lurketh about his mouth. Goeth he not along like a dancer?

Altered is Zarathustra; a child hath Zarathustra become; an awakened one is Zarathustra: what wilt thou do in the land of the sleepers?

As in the sea hast thou lived in solitude, and it hath borne thee up. Alas, wilt thou now go ashore? Alas, wilt thou again drag thy body thyself?"

Zarathustra answered: "I love mankind."

"Why," said the saint, "did I go into the forest and the desert? Was it not because I loved men far too well?

Now I love God: men, I do not love. Man is a thing too imperfect for me. Love to man would be fatal to me."

Zarathustra answered: "What spake I of love! I am bringing gifts unto men."

"Give them nothing," said the saint. "Take rather part of their load, and carry it along with them—that will be most agreeable unto them: if only it be agreeable unto thee!

If, however, thou wilt give unto them, give them no more than an alms, and let them also beg for it!"

"No," replied Zarathustra, "I give no alms. I am not poor enough for that."

The saint laughed at Zarathustra, and spake thus: "Then see to it that they accept thy treasures! They are distrustful of anchorites, and do not believe that we come with gifts.

The fall of our footsteps ringeth too hollow through their streets. And just as at night, when they are in bed and hear a man abroad long before sunrise, so they ask themselves concerning us: Where goeth the thief?

Go not to men, but stay in the forest! Go rather to the animals! Why not be like me—a bear amongst bears, a bird amongst birds?"

"And what doeth the saint in the forest?" asked Zarathustra.

The saint answered: "I make hymns and sing them; and in making hymns I laugh and weep and mumble: thus do I praise God.

With singing, weeping, laughing, and mumbling do I praise the God who is my God. But what dost thou bring us as a gift?"

When Zarathustra had heard these words, he bowed to the saint and said: "What should I have to give thee! Let me rather hurry hence lest I take aught away from thee!"—And thus they parted from one another, the old man and Zarathustra, laughing like schoolboys.

When Zarathustra was alone, however, he said to his heart: "Could it be possible! This old saint in the forest hath not yet heard of it, that GOD IS DEAD!"

3.

When Zarathustra arrived at the nearest town which adjoineth the forest, he found many people assembled in the market-place; for it had been announced that a rope-dancer would give a performance. And Zarathustra spake thus unto the people:

I TEACH YOU THE OVERMAN. Man is something that is to be surpassed. What have ye done to surpass man?

All beings hitherto have created something beyond themselves: and ye want to be the ebb of that great tide, and would rather go back to the beast than surpass man?

What is the ape to man? A laughing-stock, a thing of shame. And just the same shall man be to the Overman: a laughing-stock, a thing of shame.

Ye have made your way from the worm to man, and much within you is still worm. Once were ye apes, and even yet man is more of an ape than any of the apes.

Even the wisest among you is only a disharmony and hybrid of plant and phantom. But do I bid you become phantoms or plants?

Lo, I teach you the Overman!

The Overman is the meaning of the earth. Let your will say: The Overman SHALL BE the meaning of the earth!

I conjure you, my brethren, REMAIN TRUE TO THE EARTH, and believe not those who speak unto you of super-earthly hopes! Poisoners are they, whether they know it or not.

Despisers of life are they, decaying ones and poisoned ones themselves, of whom the earth is weary: so away with them!

Once blasphemy against God was the greatest blasphemy; but God died, and therewith also those blasphemers. To blaspheme the earth is now the dreadfulest sin, and to rate the heart of the unknowable higher than the meaning of the earth!

Once the soul looked contemptuously on the body, and then that contempt was the supreme thing:—the soul wished the body meagre, ghastly, and famished. Thus it thought to escape from the body and the earth.

Oh, that soul was itself meagre, ghastly, and famished; and cruelty was the delight of that soul!

But ye, also, my brethren, tell me: What doth your body say about your soul? Is your soul not poverty and pollution and wretched self-complacency?

Verily, a polluted stream is man. One must be a sea, to receive a polluted stream without becoming impure.

Lo, I teach you the Overman: he is that sea; in him can your great contempt be submerged.

What is the greatest thing ye can experience? It is the hour of great contempt. The hour in which even your happiness becometh loathsome unto you, and so also your reason and virtue.

The hour when ye say: "What good is my happiness! It is poverty and pollution and wretched self-complacency. But my happiness should justify existence itself!"

The hour when ye say: "What good is my reason! Doth it long for knowledge as the lion for his food? It is poverty and pollution and wretched self-complacency!"

The hour when ye say: "What good is my virtue! As yet it hath not made me passionate. How weary I am of my good and my bad! It is all poverty and pollution and wretched self-complacency! "

The hour when ye say: "What good is my justice! I do not see that I am fervour and fuel. The just, however, are fervour and fuel!"

The hour when ye say: "What good is my pity! Is not pity the cross on which he is nailed who loveth man? But my pity is not a crucifixion."

Have ye ever spoken thus? Have ye ever cried thus? Ah! would that I had heard you crying thus!

It is not your sin—it is your self-satisfaction that crieth unto heaven; your very sparingness in sin crieth unto heaven!

Where is the lightning to lick you with its tongue? Where is the frenzy with which ye should be inoculated?

Lo, I teach you the Overman: he is that lightning, he is that frenzy!—

When Zarathustra had thus spoken, one of the people called out: "We have now heard enough of the rope-dancer; it is time now for us to see him!" And all the people laughed at Zarathustra. But the rope-dancer, who thought the words applied to him, began his performance.

4.

Zarathustra, however, looked at the people and wondered. Then he spake thus:

Man is a rope stretched between the animal and the Over-man—a rope over an abyss.

A dangerous crossing, a dangerous wayfaring, a dangerous looking-back, a dangerous trembling and halting.

What is great in man is that he is a bridge and not a goal: what is lovable in man is that he is an OVER-GOING and a DOWN-GOING.

I love those that know not how to live except as down-goers, for they are the over-goers.

I love the great despisers, because they are the great adorers, and arrows of longing for the other shore.

I love those who do not first seek a reason beyond the stars for going down and being sacrifices, but sacrifice themselves to the earth, that the earth of the Overman may hereafter arrive.

I love him who liveth in order to know, and seeketh to know in order that the Overman may hereafter live. Thus seeketh he his own down-going.

I love him who laboureth and inventeth, that he may build the house for the Overman, and prepare for him earth, animal, and plant: for thus seeketh he his own down-going.

I love him who loveth his virtue: for virtue is the will to down-going, and an arrow of longing.

I love him who reserveth no share of spirit for himself, but wanteth to be wholly the spirit of his virtue: thus walketh he as spirit over the bridge.

I love him who maketh his virtue his inclination and destiny: thus, for the sake of his virtue, he is willing to live on, or live no more.

I love him who desireth not too many virtues. One virtue is more of a virtue than two, because it is more of a knot for one's destiny to cling to.

I love him whose soul is lavish, who wanteth no thanks and doth not give back: for he always bestoweth, and desireth not to keep for himself.

I love him who is ashamed when the dice fall in his favour, and who then asketh: "Am I a dishonest player?"—for he is willing to succumb.

I love him who scattereth golden words in advance of his deeds, and always doeth more than he promiseth: for he seeketh his own down-going.

I love him who justifieth the future ones, and redeemeth the past ones: for he is willing to succumb through the present ones.

I love him who chasteneth his God, because he loveth his God: for he must succumb through the wrath of his God.

I love him whose soul is deep even in the wounding, and may succumb through a small matter: thus goeth he willingly over the bridge.

I love him whose soul is so overfull that he forgetteth himself, and all things are in him: thus all things become his down-going.

I love him who is of a free spirit and a free heart: thus is his head only the bowels of his heart; his heart, however, causeth his down-going.

I love all who are like heavy drops falling one by one out of the dark cloud that lowereth over man: they herald the coming of the lightning, and succumb as heralds.

Lo, I am a herald of the lightning, and a heavy drop out of the cloud: the lightning, however, is the OVERMAN.—

5.

When Zarathustra had spoken these words, he again looked at the people, and was silent. "There they stand," said he to his heart; "there they laugh: they understand me not; I am not the mouth for these ears.

Must one first batter their ears, that they may learn to hear with their eyes? Must one clatter like kettledrums and penitential preachers? Or do they only believe the stammerer?

They have something whereof they are proud. What do they call it, that which maketh them proud? Culture, they call it; it distinguisheth them from the goatherds.

They dislike, therefore, to hear of 'contempt' of themselves. So I will appeal to their pride.

I will speak unto them of the most contemptible thing: that, however, is THE LAST MAN!"

And thus spake Zarathustra unto the people:

It is time for man to fix his goal. It is time for man to plant the germ of his highest hope. Still is his soil rich enough for it. But that soil will one day be poor and exhausted, and no lofty tree will any longer be able to grow thereon.

Alas! there cometh the time when man will no longer launch the arrow of his longing beyond man—and the string of his bow will have unlearned to whizz!

I tell you: one must still have chaos in one, to give birth to a dancing star. I tell you: ye have still chaos in you.

Alas! There cometh the time when man will no longer give birth to any star. Alas! There cometh the time of the most despicable man, who can no longer despise himself.

Lo! I show you THE LAST MAN.

"What is love? What is creation? What is longing? What is a star?"—so asketh the last man and blinketh.

The earth hath then become small, and on it there hoppeth the last man who maketh everything small. His species is ineradicable like that of the ground-flea; the last man liveth longest.

"We have discovered happiness"—say the last men, and blink thereby.

They have left the regions where it is hard to live; for they need warmth. One still loveth one's neighbour and rubbeth against him; for one needeth warmth.

Turning ill and being distrustful, they consider sinful: they walk warily. He is a fool who still stumbleth over stones or men!

A little poison now and then: that maketh pleasant dreams. And much poison at last for a pleasant death.

One still worketh, for work is a pastime. But one is careful lest the pastime should hurt one.

One no longer becometh poor or rich; both are too burdensome. Who still wanteth to rule? Who still wanteth to obey? Both are too burdensome.

No shepherd, and one herd! Every one wanteth the same; every one is equal: he who hath other sentiments goeth voluntarily into the madhouse.

"Formerly all the world was insane,"—say the subtlest of them, and blink thereby.

They are clever and know all that hath happened: so there is no end to their raillery. People still fall out, but are soon reconciled—otherwise it spoileth their stomachs.

They have their little pleasures for the day, and their little pleasures for the night, but they have a regard for health.

"We have discovered happiness,"—say the last men, and blink thereby.—

And here ended the first discourse of Zarathustra, which is also called "The Prologue": for at this point the shouting and mirth of the multitude interrupted him. "Give us this last man, O Zarathustra,"—they called out—"make us into these last men! Then will we make thee a present of the Overman!" And all the people exulted and smacked their lips. Zarathustra, however, turned sad, and said to his heart:

"They understand me not: I am not the mouth for these ears.

Too long, perhaps, have I lived in the mountains; too much have I hearkened unto the brooks and trees: now do I speak unto them as unto the goatherds.

Calm is my soul, and clear, like the mountains in the morning. But they think me cold, and a mocker with terrible jests.

And now do they look at me and laugh: and while they laugh they hate me too. There is ice in their laughter."

6.

Then, however, something happened which made every mouth mute and every eye fixed. In the meantime, of course, the rope-dancer had commenced his performance: he had come out at a little door, and was going along the rope which was stretched between two towers, so that it hung above the market-place and the people. When he was just midway across, the little door opened once more, and a gaudily-dressed fellow like a buffoon sprang out, and went rapidly after the first one. "Go on, halt-foot," cried his frightful voice, "go on, lazy-bones, interloper, sallow-face!—lest I tickle thee with my heel! What dost thou here between the towers? In the tower is the place for thee, thou shouldst be locked up; to one better than thyself thou blockest the way!"—And with every word he came nearer and nearer the first one. When, however, he was but a step behind, there happened the frightful thing which made every mouth mute and every eye fixed—he uttered a yell like a devil, and jumped over the other who was in his way. The latter, however, when he thus saw his rival triumph, lost at the same time his head and his footing on the rope; he threw his pole away, and shot downwards faster than it, like an eddy of arms and legs, into the depth. The market-place and the people were like the sea when the storm cometh on: they all flew apart and in disorder, especially where the body was about to fall.

Zarathustra, however, remained standing, and just beside him fell the body, badly injured and disfigured, but not yet dead. After a while consciousness returned to the shattered man, and he saw Zarathustra kneeling beside him. "What art thou doing there?" said he at last, "I knew long ago that the devil would trip me up. Now he draggeth me to hell: wilt thou prevent him?"

"On mine honour, my friend," answered Zarathustra, "there is nothing of all that whereof thou speakest: there is no devil and no hell. Thy soul will be dead even sooner than thy body: fear, therefore, nothing any more!"

The man looked up distrustfully. "If thou speakest the truth," said he, "I lose nothing when I lose my life. I am not much more than an animal which hath been taught to dance by blows and scanty fare."

"Not at all," said Zarathustra, "thou hast made danger thy calling; therein there is nothing contemptible. Now thou perishest by thy calling: therefore will I bury thee with mine own hands."

When Zarathustra had said this the dying one did not reply further; but he moved his hand as if he sought the hand of Zarathustra in gratitude.

7.

Meanwhile the evening came on, and the market-place veiled itself in gloom. Then the people dispersed, for even curiosity and terror become fatigued. Zarathustra, however, still sat beside the dead man on the ground, absorbed in thought: so he forgot the time. But at last it became night, and a cold wind blew upon the lonely one. Then arose Zarathustra and said to his heart:

>Verily, a fine catch of fish hath Zarathustra made to-day! It is not a man he hath caught, but a corpse.

>Sombre is human life, and as yet without meaning: a buffoon may be fateful to it.

>I want to teach men the sense of their existence, which is the Overman, the lightning out of the dark cloud—man.

>But still am I far from them, and my sense speaketh not unto their sense. To men I am still something between a fool and a corpse.

>Gloomy is the night, gloomy are the ways of Zarathustra. Come, thou cold and stiff companion! I carry thee to the place where I shall bury thee with mine own hands.

8.

When Zarathustra had said this to his heart, he put the corpse upon his shoulders and set out on his way. Yet had he not gone a hundred steps, when there stole a man up to him and whispered in his ear—and lo! he that spake was the buffoon from the tower. "Leave this town, O Zarathustra," said he, "there are too many here who hate thee. The good and just hate thee, and call thee their enemy and despiser; the believers in the orthodox belief hate thee, and call thee a danger to the multitude. It was thy good fortune to be laughed at: and verily thou spakest like a buffoon. It was thy good fortune to associate with the dead dog; by so humiliating thyself thou hast saved thy life to-day. Depart, however, from this town,—or tomorrow I shall jump over thee, a living man over a dead one." And when he had said this, the buffoon vanished; Zarathustra, however, went on through the dark streets.

At the gate of the town the grave-diggers met him: they shone their torch on his face, and, recognising Zarathustra, they sorely derided him. "Zarathustra is carrying away the dead dog: a fine thing that Zarathustra hath turned a grave-digger! For our hands are too cleanly for that roast. Will Zarathustra steal the bite from the devil? Well then, good luck to the repast! If only the devil is not a better thief than Zarathustra!—he will steal them both, he will eat them both!" And they laughed among themselves, and put their heads together.

Zarathustra made no answer thereto, but went on his way. When he had gone on for two hours, past forests and swamps, he had heard too much of the hungry howling of the wolves, and he himself became a-hungry. So he halted at a lonely house in which a light was burning.

"Hunger attacketh me," said Zarathustra, "like a robber. Among forests and swamps my hunger attacketh me, and late in the night.

"Strange humours hath my hunger. Often it cometh to me only after a repast, and all day it hath failed to come: where hath it been?"

And thereupon Zarathustra knocked at the door of the house. An old man appeared, who carried a light, and asked: "Who cometh unto me and my bad sleep?"

"A living man and a dead one," said Zarathustra. "Give me something to eat and drink, I forgot it during the day. He that feedeth the hungry refresheth his own soul, saith wisdom."

The old man withdrew, but came back immediately and offered Zarathustra bread and wine. "A bad country for the hungry," said he; "that is why I live here. Animal and man come unto me, the anchorite. But bid thy companion eat and drink also, he is wearier than thou." Zarathustra answered: "My companion is dead; I shall hardly be able to persuade him to eat." "That doth not concern me," said the old man sullenly; "he that knocketh at my door must take what I offer him. Eat, and fare ye well!"—

Thereafter Zarathustra again went on for two hours, trusting to the path and the light of the stars: for he was an experienced night-walker, and liked to look into the face of all that slept. When the morning dawned, however, Zarathustra found himself in a thick forest, and no path was any longer visible. He then put the dead man in a hollow tree at his head—for he wanted to protect him from the wolves—and laid himself down on the ground and moss. And immediately he fell asleep, tired in body, but with a tranquil soul.

9.

Long slept Zarathustra; and not only the rosy dawn passed over his head, but also the morning.

At last, however, his eyes opened, and amazedly he gazed into the forest and the stillness, amazedly he gazed into himself. Then he arose quickly, like a seafarer who all at once seeth the land; and he shouted for joy: for he saw a new truth. And he spake thus to his heart:

A light hath dawned upon me: I need companions—living ones; not dead companions and corpses, which I carry with me where I will.

But I need living companions, who will follow me because they want to follow themselves—and to the place where I will.

A light hath dawned upon me. Not to the people is Zarathustra to speak, but to companions! Zarathustra shall not be the herd's herdsman and hound!

To allure many from the herd—for that purpose have I come. The people and the herd must be angry with me: a robber shall Zarathustra be called by the herdsmen.

Herdsmen, I say, but they call themselves the good and just. Herdsmen, I say, but they call themselves the believers in the orthodox belief.

Behold the good and just! Whom do they hate most? Him who breaketh up their tables of values, the breaker, the law-breaker:—he, however, is the creator.

Behold the believers of all beliefs! Whom do they hate most? Him who breaketh up their tables of values, the breaker, the law-breaker—he, however, is the creator.

Companions, the creator seeketh, not corpses—and not herds or believers either. Fellow-creators the creator seeketh—those who grave new values on new tables.

Companions, the creator seeketh, and fellow-reapers: for everything is ripe for the harvest with him. But he lacketh the hundred sickles: so he pluckath the ears of corn and is vexed.

Companions, the creator seeketh, and such as know how to whet their sickles. Destroyers, will they be called, and despisers of good and evil. But they are the reapers and rejoicers.

Fellow-creators, Zarathustra seeketh; fellow-reapers and fellow-rejoicers, Zarathustra seeketh: what hath he to do with herds and herdsmen and corpses!

And thou, my first companion, rest in peace! Well have I buried thee in thy hollow tree; well have I hid thee from the wolves.

But I part from thee; the time hath arrived. 'Twixt rosy dawn and rosy dawn there came unto me a new truth.

I am not to be a herdsman, I am not to be a grave-digger. Not any more will I discourse unto the people; for the last time have I spoken unto the dead.

With the creators, the reapers, and the rejoicers will I associate: the rainbow will I show them, and all the stairs to the Overman.

To the lone-dwellers will I sing my song, and to the twain-dwellers; and unto him who hath still ears for the unheard, will I make the heart heavy with my happiness.

I make for my goal, I follow my course; over the loitering and tardy will I leap. Thus let my on-going be their down-going!

10.

This had Zarathustra said to his heart when the sun stood at noon-tide. Then he looked inquiringly aloft,—for he heard above him the sharp call of a bird. And behold! An eagle swept through the air in wide circles, and on it hung a serpent, not like a prey, but like a friend: for it kept itself coiled round the eagle's neck.

"They are mine animals," said Zarathustra, and rejoiced in his heart.

"The proudest animal under the sun, and the wisest animal under the sun,—they have come out to reconnoitre.

They want to know whether Zarathustra still liveth. Verily, do I still live?

More dangerous have I found it among men than among animals; in dangerous paths goeth Zarathustra. Let mine animals lead me!

When Zarathustra had said this, he remembered the words of the saint in the forest. Then he sighed and spake thus to his heart:

"Would that I were wiser! Would that I were wise from the very heart, like my serpent!

But I am asking the impossible. Therefore do I ask my pride to go always with my wisdom!

And if my wisdom should some day forsake me:—alas! it loveth to fly away!—may my pride then fly with my folly!"

Thus began Zarathustra's down-going.

Selected Writings

Sir Francis Bacon

1. On The Purpose of Science

***From the close of the author's preface to the* Instauratio Magna**

• But as these great things are not at our disposal, we here, at the entrance of our work, with the utmost humility and fervency, put forth our prayers to God, that remembering the miseries of mankind, and the pilgrimage of this life, where we pass but few days and sorrowful, he would vouchsafe through our hands, and the hands of others, to whom he has given the like mind, to relieve the human race by a new act of his bounty. We likewise humbly beseech him that what is human may not clash with what is divine; and that when the ways of the senses are opened, and a greater natural light set up in the mind, nothing of incredulity and blindness toward divine mysteries may arise; but rather that the understanding, now cleared up, and purged of all vanity and superstition, may remain entirely subject to the divine oracles, and yield to faith, the things that are faith's: and lastly, that expelling the poisonous knowledge infused by the serpent, which puffs up and swells the human mind, we may neither be wise above measure, nor go beyond the bounds of sobriety, but pursue the truth in charity.

• We now turn ourselves to men, with a few wholesome admonitions and just requests. And first, we admonish them to continue in a sense of their duty, as to divine matters; for the senses are like the sun, which displays the face of the earth, but shuts up that of the heavens: and again, that they run not into the contrary extreme, which they certainly will do, if they think an inquiry into nature any way forbid them by religion. It was not that pure and unspotted natural knowledge whereby Adam gave names to things, agreeable to their natures, which caused his fall; but an ambitious and authoritative desire of moral knowledge, to judge of good and evil, which makes men revolt

37

from God, and obey no laws but those of their own will. But for the sciences, which contemplate nature, the sacred philosopher declares, "It is the glory of God to conceal a thing, but the glory of a king to find it out." As if the Divine Being thus indulgently condescended to exercise the human mind by philosophical inquiries.

• In the next place, we advise all mankind to think of the true ends of knowledge, and that they endeavor not after it for curiosity, contention, or the sake of despising others, nor yet for profit, reputation, power, or any such inferior consideration, but solely for the occasions and uses of life; all along conducting and perfecting it in the spirit of benevolence. Our requests are—1. That men do not conceive we here deliver an opinion, but a work; and assure themselves we attempt not to found any sect or particular doctrine, but to fix an extensive basis for the service of human nature. 2. That, for their own sakes, they lay aside the zeal and prejudices of opinions, and endeavor the common good; and that being, by our assistance, freed and kept clear from the errors and hindrances of the way, they would themselves also take part of the task. 3. That they do not despair, as imagining our project for a grand restoration, or advancement of all kinds of knowledge, infinitely beyond the power of mortals to execute; while in reality, it is the genuine stop and prevention of infinite error. Indeed, as our state is mortal, and human, a full accomplishment cannot be expected in a single age, and must therefore be commended to posterity. Nor could we hope to succeed, if we arrogantly searched for the sciences in the narrow cells of the human understanding, and not submissively in the wider world. 4. In the last place, to prevent ill effects from contention, we desire mankind to consider how far they have a right to judge our performance, upon the foundations here laid down: for we reject all that knowledge which is too hastily abstracted from things, as vague, disorderly, and ill-formed; and we cannot be expected to abide by a judgment which is itself called in question.

From Book I of Novum Organum

i. MAN, as the minister and interpreter of nature, does and understands as much as his observations on the order of nature, either with regard to things or the mind, permit him, and neither knows nor is capable of more.

ii. The unassisted hand and the understanding left to itself possess but little power. Effects are produced by the means of instruments and helps, which the understanding requires no less than the hand; and as instruments either promote or regulate the motion of the hand, so those that are applied to the mind prompt or protect the understanding.

iii. Knowledge and human power are synonymous, since the ignorance of the cause frustrates the effect; for nature is only subdued by submission, and that which in contemplative philosophy corresponds with the cause in practical science becomes the rule.

From the end of Book II of Novum Organum

lii. . . . We must next, however, proceed to the supports and corrections of induction, and thence to concretes, the latent process, and latent conformations, and the other matters, which we have enumerated in their order in the twenty-first aphorism, in order that, like good and faithful guardians, we may yield up their fortune to mankind upon the emancipation and majority of their understanding; from which must necessarily follow an improvement of their estate, and an increase of their power over nature. For man, by the fall, lost at once his state of innocence, and his empire over creation, both of which can be partially recovered even in this life, the first by religion and faith, the second by the arts and sciences. For creation did not become entirely and utterly rebellious by the curse, but in consequence of the Divine decree, "in the sweat of thy brow shalt thou eat bread," she is compelled by our labors (not assuredly by our disputes or magical ceremonies), at length, to afford mankind in some degree his bread, that is to say, to supply man's daily wants.

II. On "True Induction" and the Failings of Aristotelian Science

From the preface to Novum Organum

They who have presumed to dogmatize on nature, as on some well investigated subject, either from self-conceit or arrogance, and in the professorial style, have inflicted the greatest injury on philosophy and learning. For they have tended to stifle and interrupt inquiry exactly in proportion as they have prevailed in bringing others to their opinion: and their own activity has not counterbalanced the mischief they have occasioned by corrupting and destroying that of others. They again who have entered upon a contrary course, and asserted that nothing whatever can be known, whether they have fallen into this opinion from their hatred of the ancient sophists, or from the hesitation of their minds, or from an exuberance of learning, have certainly adduced reasons for it which are by no means contemptible. They have not, however, derived their opinion from true sources, and, hurried on by their zeal and some affectation, have certainly exceeded due moderation. But the more ancient Greeks (whose writings have perished), held a more prudent mean, between the arrogance of dogmatism, and the despair of scepticism; and though too frequently intermingling complaints and indignation at the difficulty of inquiry, and the obscurity of things, and champing, as it were, the bit, have still persisted in pressing their point, and pursuing their intercourse with nature; thinking, as it seems, that the better method was not to dispute upon the very point of the possibility of anything being known, but to put it to the test of experience. Yet they themselves, by only employing the power of the understanding, have not adopted a fixed rule, but have laid their whole stress upon intense meditation, and a continual exercise and perpetual agitation of the mind.

Our method, though difficult in its operation, is easily explained. It consists in determining the degrees of certainty, while we, as it were, restore the senses to their former rank, but generally reject that operation of the mind which follows close upon the senses, and open and establish a new and certain course for the mind from the first actual perceptions of the senses themselves. This, no doubt, was the view taken by those who have assigned so much to logic; showing clearly thereby that they sought some support for the mind, and suspected its natural and spontaneous mode of action. But this is now employed too late as a remedy, when all is clearly lost, and after the mind, by the daily habit and intercourse of life, has come prepossessed with corrupted doctrines, and filled with the vainest idols. The art of logic therefore being (as we have mentioned), too late a precaution, and in no way remedying the matter, has tended more to confirm errors, than to disclose truth. Our only remaining hope and salvation is to begin the whole labor of the mind again; not leaving it to itself, but directing it perpetually from the very first, and attaining our end as it were by mechanical aid.

• • •

From Book I of Novum Organum

ix. The sole cause and root of almost every defect in the sciences is this, that while we falsely admire and extol the powers of the human mind, we do not search for its real helps.

x. The subtilty of nature is far beyond that of sense or of the understanding: so that the specious meditations, speculations, and theories of mankind are but a kind of insanity, only there is no one to stand by and observe it.

xi. As the present sciences are useless for the discovery of effects, so the present system of logic is useless for the discovery of the sciences.

xii. The present system of logic rather assists in confirming and rendering inveterate the errors founded on vulgar notions than in searching after truth, and is therefore more hurtful than useful.

xiii. The syllogism is not applied to the principles of the sciences, and is of no avail in intermediate axioms, as being very unequal to the subtilty of nature. It forces assent, therefore, and not things.

xiv. The syllogism consists of propositions; propositions of words; words are the signs of notions. If, therefore, the notions (which form the basis of the whole) be confused and carelessly abstracted from things, there is no solidity in the superstructure. Our only hope, then, is in genuine induction.

xv. We have no sound notions either in logic or physics; substance, quality, action, passion, and existence are not clear notions; much less weight, levity, density, tenuity, moisture, dryness, generation, corruption, attraction, repulsion, element, matter, form, and the like. They are all fantastical and ill-defined.

xvi. The notions of less abstract natures, as man, dog, dove, and the immediate perceptions of sense, as heat, cold, white, black, do not deceive us materially, yet even these are sometimes confused by the mutability of matter and the intermixture of things. All the rest which men have hitherto employed are errors, and improperly abstracted and deduced from things.

xvii. There is the same degree of licentiousness and error in forming axioms as in abstracting notions, and that in the first principles, which depend on common induction; still more is this the case in axioms and inferior propositions derived from syllogisms.

xviii. The present discoveries in science are such as lie immediately beneath the surface of common notions. It is necessary, however, to penetrate the more secret and remote parts of nature, in order to abstract both notions and axioms from things by a more certain and guarded method.

xix. There are and can exist but two ways of investigating and discovering truth. The one hurries on rapidly from the senses and particulars to the most general axioms, and from them, as principles and their supposed indisputable truth, derives and discovers the intermediate axioms. This is the way now in use. The other constructs its axioms from the senses and particulars, by ascending continually and gradually, till it finally arrives at the most general axioms, which is the true but unattempted way.

xx. The understanding when left to itself proceeds by the same way as that which it would have adopted under the guidance of logic, namely, the first; for the mind is fond of starting off to generalities, that it may avoid labor, and after dwelling a little on a subject is fatigued by experiment. But those evils are augmented by logic, for the sake of the ostentation of dispute.

xxi. The understanding, when left to itself in a man of a steady, patient, and reflecting disposition (especially when unimpeded by received doctrines), makes some attempt in the right way, but with little effect, since the understanding, undirected and unassisted, is unequal to and unfit for the task of vanquishing the obscurity of things.

xxii. Each of these two ways begins from the senses and particulars, and ends in the greatest generalities. But they are immeasurably different; for the one merely touches cursorily the limits of experiment and particulars, while the other runs duly and regularly through them—the one from the very outset lays down some abstract and useless generalities, the other gradually rises to those principles which are really the most common in nature.

xxiii. There is no small difference between the idols of the human mind and the ideas of the Divine mind—that is to say, between certain idle dogmas and the real stamp and impression of created objects, as they are found in nature.

xxiv. Axioms determined upon in argument can never assist in the discovery of new effects; for the subtilty of nature is vastly superior to that of argument. But axioms properly and regularly abstracted from particulars easily point out and define new particulars, and therefore impart activity to the sciences.

xxv. The axioms now in use are derived from a scanty handful, as it were, of experience, and a few particulars of frequent occurrence, whence they are of much the same dimensions or extent as their origin. And if any neglected or unknown instance occurs, the axiom is saved by some frivolous distinction, when it would be more consistent with truth to amend it.

xxvi. We are wont, for the sake of distinction, to call that human reasoning which we apply to nature the anticipation of nature (as being rash and premature), and that which is properly deduced from things the interpretation of nature.

xxvii. Anticipations are sufficiently powerful in producing unanimity, for if men were all to become even uniformly mad, they might agree tolerably well with each other.

xxviii. Anticipations again, will be assented to much more readily than interpretations, because being deduced from a few instances, and these principally of familiar occurrence, they immediately hit the understanding and satisfy the imagination; while, on the contrary, interpretations, being deduced from various subjects, and these widely dispersed, cannot suddenly strike the understanding, so that in common estimation they must appear difficult and discordant, and almost like the mysteries of faith.

xxix. In sciences founded on opinions and dogmas, it is right to make use of anticipations and logic if you wish to force assent rather than things.

xxx. If all the capacities of all ages should unite and combine and transmit their labors, no great progress will be made in learning by anticipations, because the radical errors, and those which occur in the first process of the mind, are not cured by the excellence of subsequent means and remedies.

xxxi. It is in vain to expect any great progress in the sciences by the superinducing or ingrafting new matters upon old. An instauration must be made from the very foundations, if we do not wish to revolve forever in a circle, making only some slight and contemptible progress.

xxxii. The ancient authors and all others are left in undisputed possession of their honors; for we enter into no comparison of capacity or talent, but of method, and assume the part of a guide rather than of a critic.

xxxiii. To speak plainly, no correct judgment can be formed either of our method or its discoveries by those anticipations which are now in common use; for it is not to be required of us to submit ourselves to the judgment of the very method we ourselves arraign.

xxxiv. Nor is it an easy matter to deliver and explain our sentiments; for those things which are in themselves new can yet be only understood from some analogy to what is old.

• • •

xxxviii. The idols and false notions which have already preoccupied the human understanding, and are deeply rooted in it, not only so beset men's minds that they become difficult of access, but even when access is obtained will again meet and trouble us in the instauration of the sciences, unless mankind when forewarned guard themselves with all possible care against them.

xxxix. Four species of idols beset the human mind, to which (for distinction's sake) we have assigned names, calling the first Idols of the Tribe, the second Idols of the Den, the third Idols of the Market, the fourth Idols of the Theatre.

xl. The formation of notions and axioms on the foundation of true induction is the only fitting remedy by which we can ward off and expel these idols. It is, however, of great service to point them out; for the doctrine of idols bears the same relation to the interpretation of nature as that of the confutation of sophisms does to common logic.

xli. The idols of the tribe are inherent in human nature and the very tribe or race of man; for man's sense is falsely asserted to be the standard of things; on the contrary, all the perceptions both of the senses and the mind bear reference to man and not to the universe, and the human mind resembles those uneven mirrors which impart their own properties to different objects, from which rays are emitted and distort and disfigure them.

xlii. The idols of the den are those of each individual; for everybody (in addition to the errors common to the race of man) has his own individual den or cavern, which intercepts and corrupts the light of nature, either from his own peculiar and singular disposition, or from his education and intercourse with others, or from his reading, and the authority acquired by those whom he reverences and admires, or from the different impressions produced on the mind, as it happens to be preoccupied and predisposed, or equable and tranquil, and the like; so that the spirit of man (according to its several dispositions), is variable, confused, and as it were actuated by chance; and Heraclitus said well that men search for knowledge in lesser worlds, and not in the greater or common world.

xliii. There are also idols formed by the reciprocal intercourse and society of man with man, which we call idols of the market, from the commerce and association of men with each other; for men converse by means of language, but words are formed at the will of the generality, and there arises from a bad and unapt formation of words a wonderful obstruction to the mind. Nor can the definitions and explanations with which learned men are wont to guard and protect themselves in some instances afford a complete remedy— words still manifestly force the understanding, throw everything into confusion, and lead mankind into vain and innumerable controversies and fallacies.

xliv. Lastly, there are idols which have crept into men's minds from the various dogmas of peculiar systems of philosophy, and also from the perverted rules of demonstration, and these we denominate idols of the theatre: for we regard all the systems of philosophy hitherto received or imagined, as so many plays brought out and performed, creating fictitious and theatrical worlds. Nor do we speak only of the present systems, or of the philosophy and sects of the ancients, since numerous other plays of a similar nature can be still composed and made to agree with each other, the causes of the most opposite errors being generally the same. Nor, again, do we allude merely to general systems, but also to many elements and axioms of sciences which have become inveterate by tradition, implicit credence, and neglect. We must, however, discuss each species of idols more fully and distinctly in order to guard the human understanding against them.

● ● ●

lix. The idols of the market are the most troublesome of all, those namely which have entwined themselves round the understanding from the associations of words and names. For men imagine that their reason governs words, while, in fact, words react upon the understanding; and this has rendered philosophy and the sciences sophistical and inactive. Words are generally formed in a popular sense, and define things by those broad lines which are most obvious to the vulgar mind; but when a more acute understanding or more diligent observation is anxious to vary those lines, and to adapt them more accurately to nature, words oppose it. Hence the great and solemn disputes of learned men often terminate in controversies about words and names, in regard to which it would be better (imitating the caution of mathematicians) to proceed more advisedly in the first instance, and to bring such disputes to a regular issue by definitions. Such definitions, however, cannot remedy the evil in natural and material objects, because they consist themselves of words, and these words produce others; so that we must necessarily have recourse to particular instances, and their regular series and arrangement, as we shall mention when we come to the mode and scheme of determining notions and axioms.

lx. The idols imposed upon the understanding by words are of two kinds. They are either the names of things which have no existence (for as some objects are from inattention left without a name, so names are formed by fanciful imaginations which are without an object), or they are the names of actual objects, but confused, badly defined, and hastily and irregularly abstracted from things. Fortune, the *primum mobile,* the planetary orbits, the element of fire, and the like fictions, which owe their birth to futile and false theories, are instances of the first kind. And this species of idols is removed with greater facility, because it can be exterminated by the constant refutation or the desuetude of the theories themselves.

• • •

lxii. The idols of the theatre, or of theories, are numerous, and may, and perhaps will, be still more so. For unless men's minds had been now occupied for many ages in religious and theological considerations, and civil governments (especially monarchies), had been averse to novelties of that nature even in theory (so that men must apply to them with some risk and injury to their own fortunes, and not only without reward, but subject to contumely and envy), there is no doubt that many other sects of philosophers and theorists would have been introduced, like those which formerly flourished in such diversified abundance among the Greeks. For as many imaginary theories of the heavens can be deduced from the phenomena of the sky, so it is even more easy to found many dogmas upon the phenomena of philosophy—and the plot of this our theatre resembles those of the poetical, where the plots which are invented for the stage are more consistent, elegant, and pleasurable than those taken from real history.

In general, men take for the groundwork of their philosophy either too much from a few topics, or too little from many; in either case their philosophy is founded on too narrow a basis of experiment and natural history, and decides on too scanty grounds. For the theoretic philosopher seizes various common circumstances by experiment, without reducing them to certainty or examining and frequently considering them, and relies for the rest upon meditation and the activity of his wit.

There are other philosophers who have diligently and accurately attended to a few experiments, and have thence presumed to deduce and invent systems of philosophy, forming everything to conformity with them.

A third set, from their faith and religious veneration, introduce theology and traditions; the absurdity of some among them having proceeded so far as to seek and derive the sciences from spirits and genii. There are, therefore, three sources of error and three species of false philosophy; the sophistic, empiric, and superstitious.

lxiii. Aristotle affords the most eminent instance of the first; for he corrupted natural philosophy by logic—thus he formed the world of categories, assigned to the human soul, the noblest of substances, a genus determined by words of secondary operation, treated of density and rarity (by which bodies occupy a greater or lesser space), by the frigid distinctions of action and power, asserted that there was a peculiar and proper motion in all bodies, and that if they shared in any other motion, it was owing to an external moving cause, and imposed innumerable arbitrary distinctions upon the nature of things; being everywhere more anxious as to definitions in teaching and the accuracy of the wording of his propositions, than the internal truth of things. And this is best shown by a comparison of his philosophy with the others of greatest repute among the Greeks. For the similar parts of Anaxagoras, the atoms of Leucippus and Democritus, the heaven and earth of Parmenides, the discord and concord of Empedocles, the resolution of bodies into the common nature of fire, and their condensation according to Heraclitus, exhibit some sprinkling of natural philosophy, the nature of things, and experiment; while Aristotle's physics are mere logical terms, and he remodelled the same subject in his metaphysics under a more imposing title, and more as a realist than a nominalist. Nor is much stress to be laid on his frequent recourse to experiment in his books on animals, his problems, and other treatises; for he had already decided, without having properly consulted experience as the basis of his decisions and axioms, and after having so decided, he drags experiment along as a captive constrained to accommodate herself to his decisions: so that he is even more to be blamed than his modern followers (of the scholastic school) who have deserted her altogether.

• • •

lxv. The corruption of philosophy by the mixing of it up with superstition and theology, is of a much wider extent, and is most injurious to it both as a whole and in parts. For the human understanding is no less exposed to the impressions of fancy, than to those of vulgar notions. The disputatious and sophistic school entraps the understanding, while the fanciful, bombastic, and, as it were, poetical school, rather flatters it. There is a clear example of this among the Greeks, especially in Pythagoras, where, however, the superstition is coarse and overcharged, but it is more dangerous and refined in Plato and his school. This evil is found also in some branches of other systems of philosophy, where it introduces abstracted forms, final and first causes, omitting frequently the intermediate and the like. Against it we must use the greatest caution; for the apotheosis of error is the greatest evil of all, and when folly is worshipped, it is, as it were, a plague spot upon the understanding. Yet some of the moderns have indulged this folly with such consummate inconsiderateness, that they have endeavored to build a system of natural philosophy on the first chapter of Genesis, the book of Job, and other parts of Scripture; seeking thus the dead among the living. And this folly is the more to be prevented and restrained, because not only fantastical philosophy, but heretical religion spring from the absurd mixture of matters divine and human. It is therefore most wise soberly to render unto faith the things that are faith's.

lxvi. Having spoken of the vicious authority of the systems founded either on vulgar notions, or on a few experiments, or on superstition, we must now consider the faulty subjects for contemplation, especially in natural philosophy. The human understanding is perverted by observing the power of mechanical arts, in which bodies are very materially changed by composition or separation, and is induced to suppose that something similar takes place in the universal nature of things. Hence the fiction of elements, and their co-operation in forming natural bodies. Again, when man reflects upon the entire liberty of nature, he meets with particular species of things, as animals, plants, minerals, and is thence easily led to imagine that there exist in nature certain primary forms which she strives to produce, and that all variation from them arises from some impediment or error which she is exposed to in completing her work, or from the collision or metamorphosis of different species. The first hypothesis has produced the doctrine of elementary properties, the second that of occult properties and specific powers; and both lead to trifling courses of reflection, in which the mind acquiesces, and is thus diverted from more important subjects. But physicians exercise a much more useful labor in the consideration of the secondary qualities of things, and the operations of attraction, repulsion, attenuation, inspissation, dilatation, astringency, separation, maturation, and the like; and would do still more if they would not corrupt these proper observations by the two systems I have alluded to, of elementary qualities and specific powers, by which they either reduce the secondary to first qualities, and their subtile and immeasurable composition, or at any rate neglect to advance by greater and more diligent observation to the third and fourth qualities, thus terminating their contemplation prematurely. Nor are these powers (or the like) to be investigated only among the medicines for the human body, but also in all changes of other natural bodies.

A greater evil arises from the contemplation and investigation rather of the stationary principles of things from which, than of the active by which things themselves are created. For the former only serve for discussion, the latter for practice. Nor is any value to be set on those common differences of motion which are observed in the received system of natural philosophy, as generation, corruption, augmentation, diminution, alteration, and translation. For this is their meaning: if a body, unchanged in other respects, is moved from its place, this is translation; if the place and species be given, but the quantity changed, it is alteration; but if, from such a change, the mass and quantity of the body do not continue the same, this is the motion of augmentation and diminution; if the change be continued so as to vary the species and substance, and transfuse them to others, this is generation and corruption. All this is merely popular, and by no means penetrates into nature; and these are but the measures and bounds of motion, and not different species of it; they merely suggest how far, and not how or whence. For they exhibit neither the affections of bodies nor the process of their parts, but merely establish a division of that motion, which coarsely exhibits to the senses matter in its varied form. Even when they wish to point out something relative to the causes of motion, and to establish a division of them, they most absurdly introduce natural and violent motion, which is also a popular notion, since every violent motion is also in fact natural, that is to say, the external efficient puts nature in action in a different manner to that which she had previously employed.

But if, neglecting these, any one were, for instance, to observe that there is in bodies a tendency of adhesion, so as not to suffer the unity of nature to be completely separated or broken, and a *vacuum* to be formed, or that they have a tendency to return to their natural dimensions or tension, so that, if compressed or extended within or beyond it, they immediately strive to recover themselves, and resume their former volume and extent; or that they have a tendency to congregate into masses with similar bodies—the dense, for instance, toward the circumference of the earth, the thin and rare toward that of the heavens. These and the like are true physical genera of motions, but the others are clearly logical and scholastic, as appears plainly from a comparison of the two.

Another considerable evil is, that men in their systems and contemplations bestow their labor upon the investigation and discussion of the principles of things and the extreme limits of nature, although all utility and means of action consist in the intermediate objects. Hence men cease not to abstract nature till they arrive at potential and shapeless matter, and still persist in their dissection, till they arrive at atoms; and yet were all this true, it would be of little use to advance man's estate.

• • •

civ. Nor can we suffer the understanding to jump and fly from particulars to remote and most general axioms (such as are termed the principles of arts and things), and thus prove and make out their intermediate axioms according to the supposed unshaken truth of the former. This, however, has always been done to the present time from the natural bent of the understanding, educated too, and accustomed to this very method, by the syllogistic mode of demonstration. But we can then only augur well for the sciences, when the assent shall proceed by a true scale and successive steps, without interruption or breach, from particulars to the lesser axioms, thence to the intermediate (rising one above the other), and lastly, to the most general. For the lowest axioms differ but little from bare experiment; the highest and most general (as they are esteemed at present), are notional, abstract, and of no real weight. The intermediate are true, solid, full of life, and upon them depend the business and fortune of mankind; beyond these are the really general, but not abstract, axioms, which are truly limited by the intermediate.

We must not then add wings, but rather lead and ballast to the understanding, to prevent its jumping or flying, which has not yet been done; but whenever this takes place, we may entertain greater hopes of the sciences.

• • •

cxxii. Again, it may be objected to us as being singular and harsh, that we should with one stroke and assault, as it were, banish all authorities and sciences, and that too by our own efforts, without requiring the assistance and support of any of the ancients.

Now we are aware, that had we been ready to act otherwise than sincerely, it was not difficult to refer our present method to remote ages, prior to those of the Greeks (since the sciences in all probability flourished more in their natural state, though silently, than when they were paraded with the fifes and trumpets of the Greeks); or even (in parts, at least) to some of the Greeks themselves, and to derive authority and honor from thence; as men of no family labor to raise and form nobility for themselves in some ancient line, by the help of genealogies. Trusting, however, to the evidence of facts, we reject every kind of fiction and imposture; and think it of no more consequence to our subject, whether future discoveries were known to the ancients, and set or rose according to the vicissitudes of events and lapse of ages, than it would be of importance to mankind to know whether the new world be the island of Atlantis, and known to the ancients, or be now discovered for the first time.

With regard to the universal censure we have bestowed, it is quite clear, to any one who properly considers the matter, that it is both more probable and more modest than any partial one could have been. For if the errors had not been rooted in the primary notions, some well conducted discoveries must have corrected others that were deficient. But since the errors were fundamental, and of such a nature, that men may be said rather to have neglected or passed over things, than to have formed a wrong or false judgment of them, it is little to be wondered at, that they did not obtain what they never aimed at, nor arrive at a goal which they had not determined, nor perform a course which they had neither entered upon nor adhered to.

With regard to our presumption, we allow that if we were to assume a power of drawing a more perfect straight line or circle than any one else, by superior steadiness of hand or acuteness of eye, it would lead to a comparison of talent; but if one merely assert that he can draw a more perfect line or circle with a ruler or compasses, than another can by his unassisted hand or eye, he surely cannot be said to boast of much. Now this applies not only to our first original attempt, but also to those who shall hereafter apply themselves to the pursuit. For our method of discovering the sciences merely levels men's wits, and leaves but little to their superiority, since it achieves everything by the most certain rules and demonstrations. Whence (as we have often observed), our attempt is to be attributed to fortune rather than talent, and is the offspring of time rather than of wit. For a certain sort of chance has no less effect upon our thoughts than on our acts and deeds.

• • •

cxxiv. Another objection will without doubt be made, namely, that we have not ourselves established a correct, or the best goal or aim of the sciences (the very defect we blame in others). For they will say that the contemplation of truth is more dignified and exalted than any utility or extent of effects; but that our dwelling so long and anxiously on experience and matter, and the fluctuating state of particulars, fastens the mind to earth, or rather casts it down into an abyss of confusion and disturbance, and separates and removes it from a much more divine state, the quiet and tranquillity of abstract wisdom. We willingly assent to their reasoning, and are most anxious to effect the very point they hint at and require. For we are founding a real model of the world in the understanding, such as it is found to be, not such as man's reason has distorted. Now this cannot be done without dissecting and anatomizing the world most diligently; but we declare it necessary to destroy completely the vain, little and, as it were, apish imitations of the world, which have been formed in various systems of philosophy by men's fancies. Let men learn (as we have said above) the difference that exists between the idols of the human mind and the ideas of the divine mind. The former are mere arbitrary abstractions; the latter the true marks of the Creator on his creatures, as they are imprinted on, and defined in matter, by true and exquisite touches. Truth, therefore, and utility, are here perfectly identical, and the effects are of more value as pledges of truth than from the benefit they confer on men.

cxxv. Others may object that we are only doing that which has already been done, and that the ancients followed the same course as ourselves. They may imagine, therefore, that, after all this stir and exertion, we shall at last arrive at some of those systems that prevailed among the ancients: for that they, too, when commencing their meditations, laid up a great store of instances and particulars, and digested them under topics and titles in their commonplace books, and so worked out their systems and arts, and then decided upon what they discovered, and related now and then some examples to confirm and throw light upon their doctrine; but thought it superfluous and troublesome to publish their notes, minutes, and commonplaces, and therefore followed the example of builders who remove the scaffolding and ladders when the building is finished. Nor can we indeed believe the case to have been otherwise. But to any one, not entirely forgetful of our previous observations, it will be easy to answer this objection or rather scruple; for we allow that the ancients had a particular form of investigation and discovery, and their writings show it. But it was of such a nature, that they immediately flew from a few instances and particulars (after adding some common notions, and a few generally received opinions most in vogue) to the most general conclusions or the principles of the sciences, and then by their intermediate propositions deduced their inferior conclusions, and tried them by the test of the immovable and settled truth of the first, and so constructed their art. Lastly, if some new particulars and instances were brought forward, which contradicted their dogmas, they either with great subtilty reduced them to one system, by distinctions or explanations of their own rules, or got rid of them clumsily as exceptions, laboring most pertinaciously in the meantime to accommodate the causes of such as were not contradictory to their own principles. Their natural history and their experience were both far from being what they ought to have been and their flying off to generalities ruined everything.

cxxvi. Another objection will be made against us, that we prohibit decisions and the laying down of certain principles, till we arrive regularly at generalities by the intermediate steps, and thus keep the judgment in suspense and lead to uncertainty. But our object is not uncertainty but fitting certainty, for we derogate not from the senses but assist them, and despise not the understanding but direct it. It is better to know what is necessary, and not to imagine we are fully in possession of it, than to imagine that we are fully in possession of it, and yet in reality to know nothing which we ought.

III. On Final Causality

From Book II of Novum Organum

ii. The unhappy state of man's actual knowledge is manifested even by the common assertions of the vulgar. It is rightly laid down that true knowledge is that which is deduced from causes. The division of four causes also is not amiss: matter, form, the efficient, and end or final cause. Of these, however, the latter is so far from being beneficial, that it even corrupts the sciences, except in the intercourse of man with man. The discovery of form is considered desperate. As for the efficient cause and matter (according to the present system of inquiry and the received opinions concerning them, by which they are placed remote from, and without any latent process toward form), they are but desultory and superficial, and of scarcely any avail to real and active knowledge. Nor are we unmindful of our having pointed out and corrected above the error of the human mind, in assigning the first qualities of essence to forms. For although nothing exists in nature except individual bodies, exhibiting clear individual effects according to particular laws, yet in each branch of learning, that very law, its investigation, discovery, and development, are the foundation both of theory and practice. This law, therefore, and its parallel in each science, is what we understand by the term form, adopting that word because it has grown into common use, and is of familiar occurrence.

iii. He who has learned the cause of a particular nature (such as whiteness or heat), in particular subjects only, has acquired but an imperfect knowledge: as he who can induce a certain effect upon particular substances only, among those which are susceptible of it, has acquired but an imperfect power. But he who has only learned the efficient and material cause (which causes are variable and mere vehicles conveying form to particular substances) may perhaps arrive at some new discoveries in matters of a similar nature, and prepared for the purpose, but does not stir the limits of things which are much more deeply rooted; while he who is acquainted with forms, comprehends the unity of nature in substances apparently most distinct from each other. He can disclose and bring forward, therefore (though it has never yet been done), things which neither the vicissitudes of nature, nor the industry of experiment, nor chance itself, would ever have brought about, and which would forever have escaped man's thoughts; from the discovery of forms, therefore, results genuine theory and free practice.

From Section 7 of **The Advancement of Learning**

(7) The second part of metaphysic is the inquiry of final causes, which I am moved to report not as omitted, but as misplaced. And yet if it were but a fault in order, I would not speak of it; for order is matter of illustration, but pertaineth not to the substance of sciences. But this misplacing hath caused a deficiency, or at least a great improficience in the sciences themselves. For the handling of final causes, mixed with the rest in physical inquiries, hath intercepted the severe and diligent inquiry of all real and physical causes, and given men the occasion to stay upon these satisfactory and specious causes, to the great arrest and prejudice of further discovery. For this I find done not only by Plato, who ever anchoreth upon that shore, but by Aristotle, Galen, and others which do usually likewise fall upon these flats of discoursing causes. For to say that "the hairs of the eyelids are for a quickset and fence about the sight;" or that "the firmness of the skins and hides of living creatures is to defend them from the extremities of heat or cold;" or that "the bones are for the columns or beams, whereupon the frames of the bodies of living creatures are built;" or that "the leaves of trees are for protecting of the fruit;" or that "the clouds are for watering of the earth;" or that "the solidness of the earth is for the station and mansion of living creatures;" and the like, is well inquired and collected in metaphysic, but in physic they are impertinent. Nay, they are, indeed, but *remoras* and hindrances to stay and slug the ship from further sailing; and have brought this to pass, that the search of the physical causes

hath been neglected and passed in silence. And, therefore, the natural philosophy of Democritus and some others, who did not suppose a mind or reason in the frame of things, but attributed the form thereof able to maintain itself to infinite essays or proofs of Nature, which they term fortune, seemeth to me (as far as I can judge by the recital and fragments which remain unto us) in particularities of physical causes more real and better inquired than that of Aristotle and Plato; whereof both intermingled final causes, the one as a part of theology, and the other as a part of logic, which were the favourite studies respectively of both those persons; not because those final causes are not true and worthy to be inquired, being kept within their own province, but because their excursions into the limits of physical causes hath bred a vastness and solitude in that tract. For otherwise, keeping their precincts and borders, men are extremely deceived if they think there is an enmity or repugnancy at all between them. For the cause rendered, that "the hairs about the eyelids are for the safeguard of the sight," doth not impugn the cause rendered, that "pilosity is incident to orifices of moisture— *muscosi fontes*, &c." Nor the cause rendered, that "the firmness of hides is for the armour of the body against extremities of heat or cold," doth not impugn the cause rendered, that "contraction of pores is incident to the outwardest parts, in regard of their adjacence to foreign or unlike bodies;" and so of the rest, both causes being true and compatible, the one declaring an intention, the other a consequence only. Neither doth this call in question or derogate from Divine Providence, but highly confirm and exalt it. For as in civil actions he is the greater and deeper politique that can make other men the instruments of his will and ends, and yet never acquaint them with his purpose, so as they shall do it and yet not know what they do, than he that imparteth his meaning to those he employeth; so is the wisdom of God more admirable, when Nature intendeth one thing and Providence draweth forth another, than if He had communicated to particular creatures and motions the characters and impressions of His Providence. And thus much for metaphysic; the latter part whereof I allow as extant, but wish it confined to his proper place.

from The Assayer

Galileo

The Assayer, in which are weighed with a fine and accurate balance the contents of the *Astronomical and Philosophical Weighing Scales* of Lothario Sarsi of Siguenza, written in the form of a letter to the Illustrious and Very Reverend Monsignor Don Virginio Cesarini, Lincean Academician, and Chamberlain to his Holiness, by Signor Galileo Galilei, Lincean Academician, Gentleman of Florence, and Chief Philosopher and Mathematician to the Most Serene Grand Duke of Tuscany (Rome, Giacomo Mascardi, 1623).

[The Language of Nature]

. . . . [24] I seem to detect in Sarsi a firm belief that, in philosophising, it is necessary to depend on the opinions of some famous author, as if our minds should remain completely sterile and barren, when not wedded to the reasonings of someone else. [25] Perhaps he thinks that philosophy is a book of fiction written by some man, like the *Iliad*, or *Orlando Furioso*—books in which the least important thing is whether what is written there is true. Mr. Sarsi, this is not how the matter stands. Philosophy is written in this vast book, which continuously lies upon before our eyes (I mean the universe). But it cannot be understood unless you have first learned to understand the language and recognise the characters in which it is written. It is written in the language of mathematics, and the characters are triangles, circles, and other geometrical figures. Without such means, it is impossible for us humans to understand a word of it, and to be without them is to wander around in vain through a dark labyrinth. . . .

[Primary and Secondary Qualities]

. . . . [196] It now remains for me to fulfil the promise I made Your Excellency above, and give you certain thoughts of mine about the proposition 'Motion is the cause of heat,' showing how it seems to me possible that it is true. But first I need to give some consideration to what it is that we call 'heat,' since I strongly suspect that the concept which everyone has formed of it is very far from the true one. People have come to believe that it is a genuine accident, affection, or quality, which inheres as something real in the matter which we feel ourselves being warmed by. Nevertheless, I say that, as soon as I conceive of a piece of matter, or a corporeal substance. I feel myself necessarily compelled [197] to conceive along with it, that it is bounded, and has this or that shape; that in relation to some other body it is either small or large; that it is in this or that place, and in this or that time; that it is in motion or at rest; that it either touches or does not touch some other body; and that it is one, few, or many: nor can I separate it from these states by any act of the imagination. But I do not feel my mind forced to conceive it as necessarily accompanied by such states as being white or red, bitter or sweet, noisy or quiet, or having a nice or nasty smell. On the contrary, if we were not guided by our senses, thinking or imagining would probably never arrive at them by themselves. This is why I think that, as far as concerns the subject in which these tastes, smells, colours, etc. appear to us as inhering, they are nothing other than mere names, and they inhere only in the sentient body. Consequently, if the animal were removed, all these qualities would disappear and be annihilated. But whenever we ourselves have imposed on such things individual names which are different from those of the other primary and real accidents, we want to believe that they also truly exist, and are really distinct from the latter.

I believe that a few examples will make my conception clearer. I move one of my hands, first over a marble statue, and then over a living person. As far as concerns the action which comes from the hand to each subject, it is one and the same, and it consists of those primary accidents, namely motion and touch: and these are the only names we have given them. But the animate body which is subject to these actions feels different affections depending on which parts are touched. For example, when touched under the soles of the feet, on the knees, or under the armpits, in addition to the ordinary sensation of touch, there is another sensation to which we have given a special name, by calling it 'tickling.' This affection belongs wholly to us, and not a whit of it belongs to the hand. And it seems to me that it would be a serious error if one wanted to say that, in addition to the motion and the touching, the hand had in itself this distinct capacity [198] of tickling, as if tickling were an accident which inhered in it. A little piece of paper or a feather drawn lightly over any part of our body performs intrinsically the same action throughout, namely moving and touching us; but on touching us around the eyes, the nose, or under the nostrils, it gives rise to an almost intolerable itching, whereas in other parts we scarcely feel it. This itching belongs entirely to us, and not to the feather. Remove the animate and sentient body, and it is nothing other than a mere name. I believe that many other qualities which have been attributed to natural bodies (such as tastes, smells, colours, and others) have no greater an existence.

When a body which is solid (or very 'material' as it is called) is in motion, and comes into contact with any part of my person, it produces in me the sensation which we call 'touch.' Although it is present over the whole of the body, nevertheless, it seems to reside mainly in the palms of the hands, and especially in the tips of the fingers, with which we sense the tiniest differences in roughness, smoothness, softness, and hardness, which we cannot distinguish so easily with other parts of the body. Some of these sensations are more pleasant than others, and others less pleasant, depending on the different shapes of the bodies which are touched—smooth or scaly, sharp or blunt, hard or yielding. And this sense is, as it were, more material than the others: and since it arises from the solidity of matter, it seems to be related to the element Earth.

Some of these bodies are continuously dissolving into tiny particles: and of these, some fall downwards because they are heavier than air, and other lighter ones rise upwards. This is perhaps the source of two other senses, when these particles strike two parts of our body which are much more sensitive than our skin, which cannot sense the impact of such subtle, tenuous, and tiny matter. Of these tiny particles, the ones which descend are received by the upper part of the tongue, and, penetrating into its substance by blending with its humidity, they give rise to pleasant or unpleasant tastes, depending on the different ways in which the different shapes of these tiny particles touch the tongue, and on whether they are few or many, and faster or slower. The others, which rise upwards, enter by the nostrils, and will [199] strike certain little bumps which are the organ of taste; and here they are received in a similar way, and how they touch and pass among them gives rise to pleasure or displeasure, depending on whether they have this or that shape; on whether their motion is slow or quick; and on whether they are very few, quite a few, or many. The tongue and the nasal passages seem to be providentially situated, since the former is spread out underneath to receive the impact of the descending particles, and the latter is suitable for the ones which rise. Perhaps, by a certain analogy, things of a watery nature are suitable for giving rise to tastes, since they descend in the air; whereas things with a fiery nature are suitable for smells, since they rise.

Air is the one remaining element left for sounds. These come to us indifferently from below, from above, and horizontally, since we are located in the air, and any motion in the air itself (i.e. in its proper region), is propagated equally in all directions. The position of the ears is as suitable as could possibly be for pointing them in any direction. Sounds are generated and sensed in us when (without any quality of 'sonority' or 'transonority' a rapid vibration of the air rippling into minute waves moves certain cartilages of our eardrums. There are very many ways in which external things have the power to make the air ripple like this; but perhaps they are mostly reducible to the vibration of some body which makes the air ripple by pushing against it. The waves are propagated through the air at great speed, and the greater their frequency the higher the sound they give rise to.

I do not believe that external bodies need anything more than size, shape, number, and slow or quick motion, to excite in us tastes, smells, and sounds. I think that if ears, tongues, and noses were taken away, shapes, numbers, and motions would certainly remain, but there would no longer be smells, tastes, or sounds. Without a living animal, I do not believe that these would be anything other than names just as I said above, that tickling and itching are mere names without armpits and the skin inside the nose.

Just as I have considered these four senses in relation to the four elements, so I believe that vision, which is pre-eminent above all the others, is related to light; but in a ratio [200] of excellence such as holds between the finite and the infinite: between that which takes place over time, and the instantaneous: between that which has quantity, and the indivisible; and between light and darkness. As for this sensation and its concomitant properties, I shall not pretend to Your Excellency that I understand more than a very little: and to explain this little (or more accurately, to sketch it in writing) would take more than just a long time, and so I pass it over in silence.

I now return to the proposition I originally posed in this section. We have already seen that many affections which are believed to be qualities inhering in external subjects do not have any real existence expect in ourselves, and that outside ourselves they are nothing but names. I say that I am strongly inclined to believe that heat is of the same kind, and that material things which make us hot and feel hot (such as we call by the general name 'fire') are a multitude of tiny corpuscles of such and such a shape, and moving at such and such a speed. When they meet our bodies, they penetrate them with their extreme subtlety, and the way they touch our substance as they pass through it is sensed by us as the affection we call 'heat.' It is pleasant or unpleasant in proportion to the number and speed of the particles as they prick and penetrate it. This penetration is pleasant if it is beneficial to our insensible vital functions, and unpleasant when it causes too much of a separation and dissolution of our substance.

To sum up, all that fire does in itself is to move; and with its extreme degree of subtlety, it penetrates all bodies, and it dissolves them more or less quickly, depending on the number and speed of the fire-corpuscles, or the density or rarity of the bodies. Many of these bodies are such that, as they dissolve, the larger part of them is transformed into further fiery particles, and the resolution continues as long as there is still matter capable of being broken down. But I do not believe that, apart from shape, number, motion, penetration, and touching, there is any other quality in fire; and if there is, that it is heat. In my view, heat belongs to us so exclusively that, if there were no animate and sentient body, all that would be left of heat would be a mere [201] word.

Since this affection is produced in us by the fire-corpuscles passing through and touching our substance, it is obvious that they will have no more effect when they come to a halt. When a certain amount of fire is trapped in the porosity and passages of quicklime, we see that it does not warm us, even if we hold it in our hands, because it is at rest. But if we put the stone in water, where the heaviness of the water gives it a greater propensity towards motion than it had in the air, the fire-particles escape, and when they encounter our hands, they penetrate them, and we feel the warmth.

Consequently, since the mere presence of fire-particles is not sufficient to generate heat, but it is also necessary for them to be in motion, it therefore seems to me that it was not without good reason that I said that motion is the cause of heat. This is the motion by which faggots and other kinds of wood burn: and by which lead and other metals melt. As long as the fire-particles are in motion (whether they maintain their speed by themselves, or whether, losing their own force, they are impelled by the violent blast of the bellows), they penetrate all bodies, and dissolve some of them into other flying fire corpuscles; they pulverise others into the tiniest of particles; and they liquefy others, turning them into fluids which are like water.

But I think it is a serious error to take this proposition in the ordinary sense, as if a piece of stone, or iron, or wood had to heat up because it was moving. Rather, when two hard bodies are rubbed together, the friction either breaks up their parts into very subtle and volatile particles, or it opens a way out for the fire particles inside. This finally reduces them to motion, and when they encounter our bodies, they penetrate and pass through them. The sentient soul senses their contacts as they pass through, and feels the pleasant or unpleasant affections which we have named 'warm,' 'burning,' or 'scalding.'

As long as the refining and rubbing away remains confined within the smallest particles of a finite size, their motion takes place within time, and their action only generates heat. But perhaps the ultimate and deepest level of resolution results in atoms which are indivisible in reality and light is created by their motion—or it would be better to say their instantaneous scattering and diffusion [202]. Because of its, I don't know if I should call it 'subtlety,' 'rarity,' or 'immateriality,' or some other state which is completely different from all of these, and has no name—because of this, it has the power to occupy immense tracts of space.

Your Excellency, I would not wish to become inadvertently engulfed in an infinite ocean, from which I could not get back to port. Nor would I wish, while attempting to remove one doubt, to give birth to a hundred; as I fear has partly happened, because of the little distance I have ventured from the shore. Nevertheless, I want to keep my options open for a more appropriate occasion. . . .

from **Leviathan**

Thomas Hobbes

CHAPTER XIII.

Of the Natural Condition of Mankind as Concerning Their Felicity, and Misery.

Men by nature equal.

Nature hath made men so equal, in the faculties of the body, and mind; as that though there be found one man sometimes manifestly stronger in body, or of quicker mind than another; yet when all is reckoned together, the difference between man, and man, is not so considerable, as that one man can thereupon claim to himself any benefit, to which another may not pretend, as well as he. For as to the strength of body, the weakest has strength enough to kill the strongest, either by secret machination, or by confederacy with others, that are in the same danger with himself.

And as to the faculties of the mind, setting aside the arts grounded upon words, and especially that skill of proceeding upon general, and infallible rules, called science; which very few have, and but in few things; as being not a native faculty, born with us; nor attained, as prudence, while we look after somewhat else, I find yet a greater equality amongst men, than that of strength. For prudence, is but experience; which equal time, equally bestows on all men, in those things they equally apply themselves unto. That which may perhaps make such equality incredible, is but a vain conceit of one's own wisdom, which almost all men think they have in a greater degree, than the vulgar; that is, than all men but themselves, and a few others, whom by fame, or for concurring with themselves, they approve. For such is the nature of men, that howsoever they may acknowledge many others to be more witty, or more eloquent, or more learned; yet they will hardly believe there be many so wise as themselves; for they see their own wit at hand, and other men's at a distance. But this proveth rather that men are in that point equal, than unequal. For there is not ordinarily a greater sign of the equal distribution of any thing, than that every man is contented with his share.

From equality proceeds diffidence.

From this equality of ability, ariseth equality of hope in the attaining of our ends. And therefore if any two men desire the same thing, which nevertheless they cannot both enjoy, they become enemies; and in the way to their end, which is principally their own conservation, and sometimes their delectation only, endeavour to destroy, or subdue one another. And from hence it comes to pass, that where an invader hath no more to fear, than another man's single power; if one plant, sow, build, or possess a convenient seat, others may probably be expected to come prepared with forces united, to dispossess, and deprive him, not only of the fruit of his labour, but also of his life, or liberty. And the invader again is in the like danger of another.

From diffidence war.

And from this diffidence of one another, there is no way for any man to secure himself, so reasonable, as anticipation; that is, by force, or wiles, to master the persons of all men he can, so long, till he see no other power great enough to endanger him: and this is no more than his own conservation requireth, and is generally allowed. Also because there be some, that taking pleasure in contemplating their own power in the acts of conquest, which they pursue farther than their security requires; if others, that otherwise would be glad to be at ease within modest bounds, should not by invasion increase their power, they would not be able, long time, by standing only on their defence, to subsist. And by consequence, such augmentation of dominion over men being necessary to a man's conservation, it ought to be allowed him.

Again, men have no pleasure, but on the contrary a great deal of grief, in keeping company, where there is no power able to over-awe them all. For every man looketh that his companion should value him, at the same rate he sets upon himself: and upon all signs of contempt, or undervaluing, naturally endeavours, as far as he dares, (which amongst them that have no common power to keep them in quiet, is far enough to make them destroy each other), to extort a greater value from his contemners, by damage; and from others, by the example.

So that in the nature of man, we find three principal causes of quarrel. First, competition; secondly, diffidence; thirdly, glory.

The first, maketh men invade for gain; the second, for safety; and the third, for reputation. The first use violence, to make themselves masters of other men's persons, wives, children, and cattle; the second, to defend them; the third, for trifles, as a word, a smile, a different opinion, and any other sign of undervalue, either direct in their persons, or by reflection in their kindred, their friends, their nation, their profession, or their name.

Out of civil states, there is always war of every one against every one.

Hereby it is manifest, that during the time men live without a common power to keep them all in awe, they are in that condition which is called war; and such a war, as is of every man, against every man. For war, consisteth not in battle only, or the act of fighting; but in a tract of time, wherein the will to contend by battle is sufficiently known: and therefore the notion of *time*, is to be considered in the nature of war; as it is in the nature of weather. For as the nature of foul weather, lieth not in a shower or two of rain; but in an inclination thereto of many days together: so the nature of war, consisteth not in actual fighting; but in the known disposition thereto, during all the time there is no assurance to the contrary. All other time is peace.

The incommodities of such a war.

Whatsoever therefore is consequent to a time of war, where every man is enemy to every man; the same is consequent to the time, wherein men live without other security, than what their own strength, and their own invention shall furnish them withal. In such condition, there is no place for industry; because the fruit thereof is uncertain: and consequently no culture of the earth; no navigation, nor use of the commodities that may be imported by sea; no commodious building; no instruments of moving, and removing, such things as require much force; no knowledge of the face of the earth; no account of time; no arts; no letters; no society; and which is worst of all, continual fear, and danger of violent death; and the life of man, solitary, poor, nasty, brutish, and short.

It may seem strange to some man, that has not well weighed these things; that nature should thus dissociate, and render men apt to invade, and destroy one another: and he may therefore, not trusting to this inference, made from the passions, desire perhaps to have the same confirmed by experience. Let him therefore consider with himself, when taking a journey, he arms himself, and seeks to go well accompanied; when going to sleep, he locks his doors; when even in his house he locks his chests; and this when he knows there be laws, and public officers, armed, to revenge all injuries shall be done him; what opinion he has of his fellow-subjects, when he rides armed; of his fellow citizens, when he locks his doors; and of his children, and servants, when he locks his chests. Does he not there as much accuse mankind by his actions, as I do by my words? But neither of us accuse man's nature in it. The desires, and other passions of man, are in themselves no sin. No more are the actions, that proceed from those passions, till they know a law that forbids them: which till laws be made they cannot know: nor can any law be made, till they have agreed upon the person that shall make it.

It may peradventure be thought, there was never such a time, nor condition of war as this; and I believe it was never generally so, over all the world: but there are many places, where they live so now. For the savage people in many places of America, except the government of small families, the concord whereof dependeth on natural lust, have no government at all; and live at this day in that brutish manner, as I said before. Howsoever, it may be perceived what manner of life there would be, where there were no common power to fear, by the manner of life, which men that have formerly lived under a peaceful government, use to degenerate into, in a civil war.

But though there had never been any time, wherein particular men were in a condition of war one against another; yet in all times, kings, and persons of sovereign authority, because of their independency, are in continual jealousies, and in the state and posture of gladiators; having their weapons pointing, and their eyes fixed on one another; that is, their forts, garrisons, and guns upon the frontiers of their kingdoms; and continual spies upon their neighbours; which is a posture of war. But because they uphold thereby, the industry of their subjects; there does not follow from it, that misery, which accompanies the liberty of particular men.

In such a war nothing is unjust.

To this war of every man, against every man, this also is consequent; that nothing can be unjust. The notions of right and wrong, justice and injustice have there no place. Where there is no common power, there is no law: where no law, no injustice. Force, and fraud, are in war the two cardinal virtues. Justice, and injustice are none of the faculties neither of the body, nor mind. If they were, they might be in a man that were alone in the world, as well as his senses, and passions. They are qualities, that relate to men in society, not in solitude. It is consequent also to the same condition, that there be no propriety, no dominion, no *mine* and *thine* distinct; but only that to be every man's, that he can get; and for so long, as he can keep it. And thus much for the ill condition, which man by mere nature is actually placed in; though with a possibility to come out of it, consisting partly in the passions, partly in his reason.

The passions that incline men to peace.

The passions that incline men to peace, are fear of death; desire of such things as are necessary to commodious living; and a hope by their industry to obtain them. And reason suggesteth convenient articles of peace, upon which men may be drawn to agreement. These articles, are they, which otherwise are called the Laws of Nature: whereof I shall speak more particularly, in the . . . following chapter.

CHAPTER XIV.

Of the First and Second Natural Laws, and of Contracts.

Right of nature what.

The right of nature, which writers commonly call *jus naturale*, is the liberty each man hath, to use his own power, as he will himself, for the preservation of his own nature; that is to say, of his own life; and consequently, of doing any thing, which in his own judgment, and reason, he shall conceive to be the aptest means thereunto.

Liberty what.

By liberty, is understood, according to the proper signification of the word, the absence of external impediments: which impediments, may oft take away part of a man's power to do what he would; but cannot hinder him from using the power left him, according as his judgment, and reason shall dictate to him.

A law of nature what. Difference of right and law.

A law of nature, *lex naturalis*, is a precept or general rule, found out by reason, by which a man is forbidden to do that, which is destructive of his life, or taketh away the means of preserving the same; and to omit that, by which he thinketh it may be best preserved. For though they that speak of this subject, use to confound *jus*, and *lex*, *right* and *law*: yet they ought to be distinguished; because right, consisteth in liberty to do, or to forbear; whereas law, determineth, and bindeth to one of them: so that law, and right, differ as much, as obligation, and liberty; which in one and the same matter are inconsistent.

Naturally every man has right to every thing. The fundamental law of nature.

And because the condition of man, as hath been declared in the precedent chapter, is a condition of war of every one against every one; in which case every one is governed by his own reason; and there is nothing he can make use of, that may not be a help unto him, in preserving his life against his enemies; it followeth, that in such a condition, every man has a right to every thing; even to one another's body.

And therefore, as long as this natural right of every man to every thing endureth, there can be no security to any man, how strong or wise soever he be, of living out the time, which nature ordinarily alloweth men to live. And consequently it is a precept, or general rule of reason, *that every man, ought to endeavour peace, as far as he has hope of obtaining it; and when he cannot obtain it, that he may seek, and use, all helps, and advantages of war.* The first branch of which rule, containeth the first, and fundamental law of nature; which is, to *seek peace, and follow it.* The second, the sum of the right of nature; which is, *by all means we can, to defend ourselves.*

The second law of nature.

From this fundamental law of nature, by which men are commanded to endeavour peace, is derived this second law; *that a man be willing, when others are so too, as far-forth, as for peace, and defence of himself he shall think it necessary, to lay down this right to all things; and be contented with so much liberty against other men, as he would allow other men against himself.* For as long as every man holdeth this right, of doing any thing he liketh; so long are all men in the condition of war. But if other men will not lay down their right, as well as he; then there is no reason for any one, to divest himself of his: for that were to expose himself to prey, which no man is bound to, rather than to dispose himself to peace. This is that law of the Gospel; *whatsoever you require that others should do to you, that do ye to them.* And that law of all men, *quod tibi fieri non vis, alteri ne feceris.*

What it is to lay down a right.

To *lay* down a man's *right* to any thing, is to *divest* himself of the *liberty*, of hindering another of the benefit of his own right to the same. For he that renounceth, or passeth away his right, giveth not to any other man a right which he had not before; because there is nothing to which every man had not right by nature: but only standeth out of his way, that he may enjoy his own original right, without hindrance from him; not without hindrance from another. So that the effect which redoundeth to one man, by another man's defect of right, is but so much diminution of impediments to the use of his own right original.

Renouncing a right, what it is. Transferring right what.
Obligation. Duty. Injustice.

Right is laid aside, either by simply renouncing it; or by transferring it to another. By *simply* renouncing; when he cares not to whom the benefit thereof redoundeth.

By transferring; when he intendeth the benefit thereof to some certain person, or persons. And when a man hath in either manner abandoned, or granted away his right; then is he said to be obliged, or bound, not to hinder those, to whom such right is granted, or abandoned, from the benefit of it: and that he *ought*, and it is his duty, not to make void that voluntary act of his own: and that such hindrance is injustice, and injury, as being *sine jure;* the right being before renounced, or transferred. So that *injury,* or *injustice,* in the controversies of the world, is somewhat like to that, which in the disputations of scholars is called *absurdity.* For as it is there called an absurdity, to contradict what one maintained in the beginning: so in the world, it is called injustice, and injury, voluntarily to undo that, which from the beginning he had voluntarily done. The way by which a man either simply renounceth, or transferreth his right, is a declaration, or signification, by some voluntary and sufficient sign, or signs, that he doth so renounce, or transfer; or hath so renounced, or transferred the same, to him that accepteth it. And these signs are either words only, or actions only; or, as it happeneth most often, both words, and actions. And the same are the bonds, by which men are bound, and obliged: bonds, that have their strength, not from their own nature, for nothing is more easily broken than a man's word, but from fear of some evil conseuence upon the rupture.

Not all rights are alienable.

Whensoever a man transferreth his right, or renounceth it; it is either in consideration of some right reciprocally transferred to himself; or for some other good he hopeth for thereby. For it is a voluntary act: and of the voluntary acts of every man, the object is some *good to himself.* And therefore there be some rights, which no man can be understood by any words, or other signs, to have abandoned, or transferred. As first a man cannot lay down the right of resisting them, that assault him by force, to take away his life; because he cannot be understood to aim thereby, at any good to himself. The same may be said of wounds, and chains, and imprisonment; both because there is no benefit consequent to such patience; as there is to the patience of suffering another to be wounded, or imprisoned: as also because a man cannot tell, when he seeth men proceed against him by violence, whether they intend his death or not. And lastly the motive, and end for which this renouncing, and transferring of right is introduced, is nothing else but the security of a man's person, in his life, and in the means of so preserving life, as not to be weary of it. And therefore if a man by words, or other signs, seem to despoil himself of the end, for which those signs were intended; he is not to be understood as if he meant it, or that it was his will; but that he was ignorant of how such words and actions were to be interpreted.

Contract what.

The mutual transferring of right, is that which men call contract.

There is difference between transferring of right to the thing; and transferring, or tradition, that is delivery of the thing itself. For the thing may be delivered together with the translation of the right; as in buying and selling with ready-money; or exchange of goods, or lands: and it may be delivered some time after.

Convenant what.

Again, one of the contractors, may deliver the thing contracted for on his part, and leave the other to perform his part at some determinate time after, and in the mean time be trusted; and then the contract on his part, is called pact, or covenant: or both parts may contract now, to perform hereafter: in which cases, he that is to perform in time to come, being trusted, his performance is called *keeping of promise,* or faith; and the failing of performance, if it be voluntary, *violation of faith.*

Free-gift.

When the transferring of right, is not mutual: but one of the parties transferred, in hope to gain thereby friendship, or service from another, or from his friends; or in hope to gain the reputation of charity, or magnanimity; or to deliver his mind from the pain of compassion; or in hope of reward in heaven; this is not contract, but gift, free-gift, grace: which words signify one and the same thing.

Signs of contract express. Promise.

Signs of contract, are either *express,* or by *inference.* Express, are words spoken with understanding of what they signify: and such words are either of the time *present,* or *past;* as, *I give, I grant, I have given, I have granted, I will that this be yours:* or of the future; as, *I will give, I will grant:* which words of the future are called promise.

Signs of contract by inference.

Signs by inference, are sometimes the consequence of words; sometimes the consequence of silence; sometimes the consequence of actions; sometimes the consequence of forbearing an action: and generally a sign by inference, of any contract, is whatsoever sufficiently argues the will of the contractor.

Free gift passeth by words of the present or past.

Words alone, if they be of the time to come, and contain a bare promise, are an insufficient sign of a free-gift, and therefore not obligatory. For if they be of the time to come, as *to-morrow I will give,* they are a sign I have not given yet, and consequently that my right is not transferred, but remaineth till I transfer it by some other act. But if the words be of the time present, or past, as, *I have given,* or, *do give to be delivered to-morrow,* then is my to-morrow's right given away to day; and that by the virtue of the words, though there were no other argument of my will. And there is a great difference in the signification of these words, *volo hoc tuum esse cras,* and *cras dabo;* that is, between *I will that this be thine to-morrow,* and, *I will give it thee to-morrow:* for the word *I will,* in the former manner of speech, signifies an act of the will present; but in the latter, it signifies a promise of an act of the will to come: and therefore the former words, being of the present, transfer a future right; the latter, that be of the future, transfer nothing. But if there be other signs of the will to transfer a right, besides words; then, though the gift be free, yet may the right be understood to pass by words of the future: as if a man propound a prize to him that comes first to the end of a race, the gift is free; and though the words be of the future, yet the right passeth: for if he would not have his words so be understood, he should not have let them run.

Signs of contract are words both of the past, present, and future.

In contracts, the right passeth, not only where the words are of the time present, or past, but also where they are of the future: because all contract is mutual translation, or change of right; and therefore he that promiseth only, because he hath already received the benefit for which he promiseth, is to be understood as if he intended the right should pass: for unless he had been content to have his words so understood, the other would not have performed his part first. And for that cause, in buying, and selling, and other acts of contract, a promise is equivalent to a covenant; and therefore obligatory.

• • •

Covenants of mutual trust, when invalid.

If a covenant be made, wherein neither of the parties perform presently, but trust one another; in the condition of mere nature, which is a condition of war of every man against every man, upon any reasonable suspicion, it is void: but if there be a common power set over them both, with right and force sufficient to compel performance, it is not void. For he that performeth first, has no assurance the other will perform after; because the bonds of words are too weak to bridle men's ambition, avarice, anger, and other passions, without the fear of some coercive power; which in the condition of mere nature, where all men are equal, and judges of the justness of their own fears, cannot possibly be supposed. And therefore he which performeth first, does but betray himself to his enemy; contrary to the right, he can never abandon, of defending his life, and means of living.

But in a civil estate, where there is a power set up to constrain those that would otherwise violate their faith, that fear is no more reasonable; and for that cause, he which by the covenant is to perform first, is obliged so to do.

The cause of fear, which maketh such a covenant invalid, must be always something arising after the covenant made; as some new fact, or other sign of the will not to perform: else it cannot make the covenant void. For that which could not hinder a man from promising, ought not to be admitted as a hindrance of performing.

Right to the end, containeth right to the means.

He that transferreth any right, transferreth the means of enjoying it, as far as lieth in his power. As he that selleth land, is understood to transfer the herbage, and whatsoever grows upon it: nor can he that sells a mill turn away the stream that drives it. And they that give to a man the right of government in sovereignty, are understood to give him the right of levying money to maintain soldiers; and of appointing magistrates for the administration of justice.

No covenant with beasts.

To make covenants with brute beasts, is impossible; because not understanding our speech, they understand not, nor accept of any translation of right; nor can translate any right to another: and without mutual acceptation, there is no covenant.

Nor with God without special revelation.

To make covenant with God, is impossible, but by mediation of such as God speaketh to, either by revelation supernatural, or by his lieutenants that govern under him, and in his name: for otherwise we know not whether our covenants be accepted, or not. And therefore they that vow anything contrary to any law of nature, vow in vain; as being a thing unjust to pay such vow.

And if it be a thing commanded by the law of nature, it is not the vow, but the law that binds them.

No covenant, but of possible and future.

The matter, or subject of a covenant, is always something that falleth under deliberation; for to covenant, is an act of the will; that is to say, an act, and the last act of deliberation; and is therefore always understood to be something to come; and which is judged possible for him that covenanteth, to perform.

And therefore, to promise that which is known to be impossible, is no covenant. But if that prove impossible afterwards, which before was thought possible, the covenant is valid, and bindeth, though not to the thing itself, yet to the value; or, if that also be impossible, to the unfeigned endeavour of performing as much as is possible: for to more no man can be obliged.

Covenants how made void.

Men are freed of their covenants two ways; by performing; or by being forgiven. For performance, is the natural end of obligation; and forgiveness, the restitution of liberty; as being a retransferring of that right, in which the obligation consisted.

Covenants extorted by fear are valid.

Covenants entered into by fear, in the condition of mere nature, are obligatory. For example, if I covenant to pay a ransom, or service for my life, to an enemy; I am bound by it: for it is a contract, wherein one receiveth the benefit of life; the other is to receive money, or service for it; and consequently, where no other law, as in the condition of mere nature, forbiddeth the performance, the covenant is valid. Therefore prisoners of war, if trusted with the payment of their ransom, are obliged to pay it: and if a weaker prince, make a disadvantageous peace with a stronger, for fear; he is bound to keep it; unless, as hath been said before, there ariseth some new, and just cause of fear, to renew the war. And even in commonwealths, if I be forced to redeem myself from a thief by promising him money, I am bound to pay it, till the civil law discharge me. For whatsoever I may lawfully do without obligation, the same I may lawfully covenant to do through fear: and what I lawfully covenant, I cannot lawfully break.

The former covenant to one, makes void the later to another.

A former covenant, makes void a later. For a man that hath passed away his right to one man today, hath it not to pass to-morrow to another: and therefore the later promise passeth no right, but is null.

A man's covenant not to defend himself is void.

A covenant not to defend myself from force, by force, is always void. For, as I have showed before, no man can transfer, or lay down his right to save himself from death, wounds, and imprisonment, the avoiding whereof is the only end of laying down any right; and therefore the promise of not resisting force, in no covenant transferreth any right; nor is obliging. For though a man may covenant thus, *unless I do so, or so, kill me;* he cannot covenant thus, *unless I do so, or so, I will not resist you, when you come to kill me.* For man by nature chooseth the lesser evil, which is danger of death in resisting; rather than the greater, which is certain and present death in not resisting. And this is granted to be true by all men, in that they lead criminals to execution, and prison, with armed men, notwithstanding that such criminals have consented to the law, by which they are condemned.

No man obliged to accuse himself.

A covenant to accuse oneself, without assurance of pardon, is likewise invalid. For in the condition of nature, where every man is judge, there is no place for accusation: and in the civil state, the accusation is followed with punishment; which being force, a man is not obliged not to resist. The same is also true, of the accusation of those, by whose condemnation a man falls into misery; as of a father, wife, or benefactor. For the testimony of such an accuser, if it be not willingly given, is presumed to be corrupted by nature; and therefore not to be received: and where a man's testimony is not to be credited, he is not bound to give it. Also accusations upon torture, are not to be reputed as testimonies. For torture is to be used but as means of conjecture, and light, in the further examination, and search of truth: and what is in that case confessed, tendeth to the ease of him that is tortured; not to the informing of the torturers: and therefore ought not to have the credit of a sufficient testimony: for whether he deliver himself by true, or false accusation, he does it by the right of preserving his own life.

The end of an oath. The form of an oath.

The force of words, being, as I have formerly noted, too weak to hold men to the performance of their covenants; there are in man's nature, but two imaginable helps to strengthen it. And those are either a fear of the consequence of breaking their word; or a glory, or pride in appearing not to need to break it. This latter is a generosity too rarely found to be presumed on, especially in the pursuers of wealth, command, or sensual pleasure; which are the greatest part of mankind. The passion to be reckoned upon, is fear; whereof there be two very general objects: one, the power of spirits invisible; the other, the power of those men they shall therein offend. Of these two, though the former be the greater power, yet the fear of the latter is commonly the greater fear. The fear of the former is in every man, his own religion: which hath place in the nature of man before civil society. The latter hath not so; at least not place enough, to keep men to their promises; because in the condition of mere nature, the inequality of power is not discerned, but by the event of battle. So that before the time of civil society, or in the interruption thereof by war, there is nothing can strengthen a covenant of peace agreed on, against the temptations of avarice, ambition, lust, or other strong desire, but the fear of that invisible power, which they every one worship as God; and fear as a revenger of their perfidy. All therefore that can be done between two men not subject to civil power, is to put one another to swear by the God he feareth: which *swearing,* or oath, is a *form of speech, added to a promise; by which he that promiseth, signifieth, that unless he perform, he renounceth the mercy of his God, or calleth to him for vengeance on himself.* Such was the heathen form, *Let* Jupiter *kill me else, as I kill this beast.* So is our form, *I shall do thus, and thus, so help me God.* And this, with the rites and ceremonies, which every one useth in his own religion, that the fear of breaking faith might be the greater.

No oath but by God.

By this it appears, that an oath taken according to any other form, or rite, than his, that sweareth, is in vain: and no oath: and that there is no swearing by any thing which the swearer thinks not God. For though men have sometimes used to swear by their kings, for fear, or flattery; yet they would have it thereby understood, they attributed to them divine honour. And that swearing unnecessarily by God, is but prophaning of his name: and swearing by other things, as men do in common discourse, is not swearing, but an impious custom, gotten by too much vehemence of talking.

An oath adds nothing to the obligation.

It appears also, that the oath adds nothing to the obligation. For a covenant, if lawful, binds in the sight of God, without the oath, as much as with it: if unlawful, bindeth not at all; though it be confirmed with an oath.

from **Pensees**

Blaise Pascal

The Wager

Infinite, nothing.—The soul of man is cast into the body, in which it finds number, time, dimension; it reasons thereon, and calls this nature or necessity, and cannot believe aught else.

Unity joined to infinity increases it not, any more than a foot measure added to infinite space. The finite is annihilated in presence of the infinite and becomes simply nought. Thus our intellect before God, thus our justice before the divine justice. There is not so great a disproportion between our justice and that of God, as between unity and infinity.

The justice of God must be as vast as his mercy, but justice towards the reprobate is less vast, and should be less amazing than mercy towards the elect.

We know that there is an infinite, but are ignorant of its nature. As we know it to be false that numbers are finite, it must therefore be true that there is an infinity in number, but what this is we know not. It can neither be odd nor even, for the addition of an unit can make no change in the nature of number; yet it is a number, and every number is either odd or even, at least this is understood of every finite number.

Thus we may well know that there is a God, without knowing what he is.

We know then the existence and the nature of the finite, because we also are finite and have dimension.

We know the existence of the infinite, and are ignorant of its nature, because it has dimension like us, but not limits like us. But we know neither the existence nor the nature of God, because he has neither dimension nor limits.

But by faith we know his existence, by glory we shall know his nature. Now I have already shown that we can know well the existence of a thing without knowing its nature.

Let us now speak according to the light of nature.

If there be a God, he is infinitely incomprehensible, since having neither parts nor limits he has no relation to us. We are then incapable of knowing either what he is or if he is. This being so, who will dare to undertake the solution of the question? Not we, who have no relation to him.

Who then will blame Christians for not being able to give a reason for their faith; those who profess a religion for which they cannot give a reason? They declare in putting it forth to the world that it is a foolishness, stultitiam, and then you complain that they do not prove it. Were they to prove it they would not keep their word, it is in lacking proof that they are not lacking in sense.

> —Yes, but although this excuses those who offer it as such, and takes away from them the blame of putting it forth without reason, it does not excuse those who receive it.

Let us then examine this point, and say, "God is, or he is not." But to which side shall we incline? Reason can determine nothing about it. There is an infinite gulf fixed between us. A game is playing at the extremity of this infinite distance in which heads or tails may turn up. What will you wager? There is no reason for backing either one or the other, you cannot reasonably argue in favour of either.

Do not then accuse of error those who have already chosen, for you know nothing about it.

> —No, but I blame them for having made, not this choice, but a choice, for again both the man who calls 'heads' and his adversary are equally to blame, they are both in the wrong; the true course is not to wager at all.

Yes, but you must wager; this depends not on your will, you are embarked in the affair. Which will you choose? Let us see. Since you must choose, let us see which least interests you. You have two things to lose, truth and good, and two things to stake, your reason and your will, your knowledge and your happiness; and your nature has two things to avoid, error and misery. Since you must needs choose, your reason is no more wounded in choosing one than the other. Here is one point cleared up, but what of your happiness? Let us weigh the gain and the loss in choosing heads that God is. Let us weigh the two cases: if you gain, you gain all; if you lose, you lose nothing. Wager then unhesitatingly that he is.

—You are right. Yes, I must wager, but I may stake too much.

Let us see. Since there is an equal chance of gain and loss, if you had only to gain two lives for one, you might still wager. But were there three of them to gain, you would have to play, since needs must that you play, and you would be imprudent, since you must play, not to chance your life to gain three at a game where the chances of loss or gain are even. But there is an eternity of life and happiness. And that being so, were there an infinity of chances of which one only would be for you, you would still be right to stake one to win two, and you would act foolishly, being obliged to play, did you refuse to stake one life against three at a game in which out of an infinity of chances there be one for you, if there were an infinity of an infinitely happy life to win. But there is here an infinity of an infinitely happy life to win, a chance of gain against a finite number of chances of loss, and what you stake is finite; that is decided. Wherever the infinite exists and there is not an infinity of chances of loss against that of gain, there is no room for hesitation, you must risk the whole. Thus when a man is forced to play he must renounce reason to keep life, rather than hazard it for infinite gain, which is as likely to happen as the loss of nothingness.

For it is of no avail to say it is uncertain that we gain, and certain that we risk, and that the infinite distance between the certainty of that which is staked and the uncertainty of what we shall gain, equals the finite good which is certainly staked against an uncertain infinite. This is not so. Every gambler stakes a certainty to gain an uncertainty, and yet he stakes a finite certainty against a finite uncertainty without acting unreasonably. It is false to say there is infinite distance between the certain stake and the uncertain gain. There is in truth an infinity between the certainty of gain and the certainty of loss. But the uncertainty of gain is proportioned to the certainty of the stake, according to the proportion of chances of gain and loss, and if therefore there are as many chances on one side as on the other, the game is even. And thus the certainty of the venture is equal to the uncertainty of the winnings, so far is it from the truth that there is infinite distance between them. So that our argument is of infinite force, if we stake the finite in a game where there are equal chances of gain and loss, and the infinite is the winnings. This is demonstrable, and if men are capable of any truths, this is one.

> —I confess and admit it. Yet is there no means of seeing the hands at the game?

Yes, the Scripture and the rest, etc.

> —Well, but my hands are tied and my mouth is gagged: I am forced to wager and am not free, none can release me, but I am so made that I cannot believe. What then would you have me do?

True. But understand at least your incapacity to believe, since your reason leads you to belief and yet you cannot believe. Labour then to convince yourself, not by increase of the proofs of God, but by the diminution of your passions. You would fain arrive at faith, but know not the way; you would heal yourself of unbelief, and you ask remedies for it. Learn of those who have been bound as you are, but who now stake all that they possess; these are they who know the way you would follow, who are cured of a disease of which you would be cured. Follow the way by which they began, by making believe that they believed, taking the holy water, having masses said, etc. Thus you will naturally be brought to believe, and will lose your acuteness.

> —But that is just what I fear.

Why? what have you to lose?

But to show you that this is the right way, this it is that will lessen the passions, which are your great obstacles, etc.

> —What you say comforts and delights me, etc.

If my words please you, and seem to you cogent, know that they are those of one who has thrown himself on his knees before and after to pray that Being, infinite, and without parts, to whom he submits all his own being, that you also would submit to him all yours, for your own good and for his glory, and that this strength may be in accord with this weakness.

The end of this argument.—Now what evil will happen to you in taking this side? You will be trustworthy, honourable, humble, grateful, generous, friendly, sincere, and true. In truth you will no longer have those poisoned pleasures, glory and luxury, but you will have other pleasures. I tell you that you will gain in this life, at each step you make in this path you will see so much certainty of gain, so much nothingness in what you stake, that you will know at last that you have wagered on a certainty, an infinity, for which you have risked nothing.

• • •

If we ought to do nothing save on a certainty, we ought to do nothing for Religion, for this is not certain. But how much we do on an uncertainty, as sea voyages, battles! I say then if this be the case we ought to do nothing at all, for nothing is certain, and that there is more certainty in Religion than that we shall see another day, for it is not certain that we shall see to-morrow, but it is certainly possible that we shall not see it. We cannot say so much about Religion. It is not certain that it is, but who will dare to say that it is certainly possible that it is not? But when we work for to-morrow, therefore for the uncertain, we act reasonably.

For we should work for the uncertain by the doctrine of chances already laid down.

Reason and the Heart

110.

We know truth, not only by the reason, but also by the heart, and it is from this last that we know first principles; and reason, which has nothing to do with it, tries in vain to combat them. The sceptics who desire truth alone labour in vain. We know that we do not dream, although it is impossible to prove it by reason, and this inability shows only the weakness of our reason, and not, as they declare, the general uncertainty of our knowledge. For our knowledge of first principles, as space, time, motion, number, is as distinct as any principle derived from reason. And reason must lean necessarily on this instinctive knowledge of the heart, and must found on it every process. We know instinctively that there are three dimensions in space, and that numbers are infinite, and reason then shows that there are no two square numbers one of which is double of the other. We feel principles, we infer propositions, both with certainty, though by different ways. It is as useless and absurd for reason to demand from the heart proofs of first principles before it will admit them, as it would be for the heart to ask from reason a feeling of all the propositions demonstrated before accepting them.

This inability should serve then only to humiliate reason, which would fain judge of all things, but not to shake our certainty, as if only reason were able to instruct us. Would to God, on the contrary, that we never needed reason, and that we knew every thing by instinct and feeling! But nature has denied us this advantage, and has on the contrary given us but little knowledge of this kind, all the rest can be acquired by reason only.

Therefore those to whom God has given Religion by an instinctive feeling, are very blessed, and justly convinced. But to those who have it not we can give it only by reasoning, waiting for the time when God shall impress it on their hearts, without which faith is human only, and useless for salvation.

423.

The heart has its reasons, which reason knows not, as we feel in a thousand instances. I say that the heart loves the universal Being naturally, and itself naturally, according as it gives itself to each, and it hardens itself against one or the other at its own will. You have rejected one and kept the other, does reason cause your love?

424.

It is the heart which is conscious of God, not the reason. This then is faith; God sensible to the heart, not to the reason.

Reason acts slowly and with so many views, on so many principles, which it ought always to keep before it, that it constantly slumbers and goes astray, from not having its principles at hand. The heart does not act thus, it acts in a moment, and is always ready to act. We must then place our faith in the heart, or it will be always vacillating.

Men often mistake their imagination for their heart, and they believe they are converted as soon as they think of being converted.

Those who are accustomed to judge by the heart do not understand the process of reasoning, for they wish to understand at a glance, and are not accustomed to seek for principles. And others on the contrary, who are accustomed to reason by principles, do not at all understand the things of the heart, seeking principles and not being able to see at a glance.

The Limits of Reason

45.

Man is only a subject full of natural error, which is indelible without grace. Nothing shows him the truth, everything deceives him. These two principles of truth, reason and the senses, in addition to the fact that they are both wanting in sincerity, reciprocally deceive each other. The senses trick the reason by false appearances, and gain from reason in their turn the same deception with which they deceive; reason avenges herself. The passions of the soul trouble the senses, and make on them false impressions. They lie and deceive, outvieing one another.

But beyond those errors which come by accident, and by a lack of intelligence, with these heterogeneous faculties. . . .

48.

The spirit of this sovereign judge of the world is not so independent but that it is liable to be troubled by the first disturbance about him. The noise of a cannon is not needed to break his train of thought, it need only be the creaking of a weathercock or a pulley. Do not be astonished if at this moment he argues incoherently, a fly is buzzing about his ears, and that is enough to render him incapable of sound judgment. Would you have him arrive at truth, drive away that creature which holds his reason in check, and troubles that powerful intellect which gives laws to towns and kingdoms. Here is a droll kind of god! O ridicolosissimo eroe! [Most ridiculous hero!]

131.

. . . I pause at the only strong point of the dogmatists, namely, that speaking sincerely and in good faith we cannot doubt of natural principles.

Against this the sceptics set in one word the uncertainty of our origin, which includes that of our nature. Which the dogmatists have been trying to answer ever since the world began.

So then war is opened among men, in which each must take a side, ranging himself either for dogmatism or for scepticism, since neutrality, which is the part of the wise, is the oldest dogma of the sceptical sect. Whoever thinks to remain neutral is before all things a sceptic. This neutrality is the essence of the sect; who is not against them is pre-eminently for them. They are not for themselves, they are neutral, indifferent, in suspense as to all things, themselves included.

What then shall man do in such a state? Shall he doubt of all, doubt whether he wake, whether you pinch him, or burn him, doubt whether he doubts, doubt whether he is? We cannot go so far as that, and I therefore state as a fact that there never has been a perfect finished sceptic; nature upholds the weakness of reason, and prevents its wandering to such a point.

Shall he say on the contrary that he is in sure possession of truth, when if we press him never so little, he can produce no title, and is obliged to quit his hold?

What a chimaera then is man! how strange and monstrous! a chaos, a contradiction, a prodigy. Judge of all things, yet a weak earth-worm; depositary of truth, yet a cesspool of uncertainty and error; the glory and offscouring of the Universe.

Who will unravel such a tangle? This is certainly beyond the power of dogmatism and scepticism, and all human philosophy. Man is incomprehensible by man. We grant to the sceptics what they have so loudly asserted, that truth is not within our reach nor to our taste, that her home is not on earth but in heaven, that she dwells within the breast of God, and that we can only know her so far as it pleases him to reveal her. Let us then learn our true nature from truth uncreate and incarnate.

Nature confounds the sceptics, and reason the dogmatists. What then will become of you, O men! who by your natural reason search out your true condition? You can neither avoid both these sects nor live in either.

Know then, proud man, how great a paradox thou art to thyself. Bow down thyself, weak reason; be silent, thou foolish nature; learn that man is altogether incomprehensible by man, and learn from your master your true condition which you ignore. Hear God.

For in a word, had man never been corrupt he would innocently and securely enjoy truth and happiness. And had man never been other than corrupt he would have no idea of virtue or blessedness. But wretched as we are, and even more than if there were no greatness in our condition, we have an idea of happiness and cannot attain it, we feel an image of truth and possess a lie only, alike incapable of absolute ignorance and of certain knowledge, so manifest is it that we once were in a degree of perfection from which we have unhappily fallen!

Yet it is an astonishing thing that the mystery most removed from our knowledge, that of the transmission of sin, should be a thing without which we can have no knowledge of ourselves. For it is certain that nothing more shocks our reason than to say that the sin of the first man rendered those culpable, who, being so distant from the source, seem incapable of participation in it. This transfusion does not only seem to us impossible, but even most unjust, for there is nothing so repugnant to the rules of our miserable justice as to damn eternally an infant incapable of will, for a sin in which he seems to have so scanty a share, that it was committed six thousand years before he was in being. Certainly nothing shocks us more rudely than this doctrine, and yet without this mystery, the most incomprehensible of all, we are incomprehensible to ourselves. The tangle of our condition takes its plies and folds in this abyss, so that man is more inconceivable without the mystery than the mystery is inconceivable to man.

Whence it appears that God, willing to render the difficulty of our being unintelligible to us, has concealed the knot so high, or rather so low, that we cannot reach it; so that it is not by the arrogant exertion of our reason, but by the simple submission of reason, that we can truly know ourselves.

from Language, Truth & Logic

A. J. Ayer

Chapter 1
The Elimination of Metaphysics
p. 35

The criterion which we use to test the genuineness of apparent statements of fact is the criterion of verifiability. We say that a sentence is factually significant to any given person, if, and only if, he knows how to verify the proposition which it purports to express—that is, if he knows what observations would lead him, under certain conditions, to accept the proposition as being true, or reject it as being false. If, on the other hand, the putative proposition is of such a character that the assumption of its truth, or falsehood, is consistent with any assumption whatsoever concerning the nature of his future experience, then, as far as he is concerned, it is, if not a tautology, a mere pseudo-proposition. The sentence expressing it may be emotionally significant to him; but it is not literally significant. And with regard to questions the procedure is the same. We inquire in every case what observations would lead us to answer the question, one way or the other; and, if none can be discovered, we must conclude that the sentence under consideration does not, as far as we are concerned, express a genuine question, however strongly its grammatical appearance may suggest that it does.

Chapter 6
Critique of Ethics and Theology
pp. 102–109

There is still one objection to be met before we can claim to have justified our view that all synthetic propositions are empirical hypotheses. This objection is based on the common supposition that our speculative knowledge is of two distinct kinds—that which relates to questions of empirical fact, and that which relates to questions of value. It will be said that "statements of value" are genuine synthetic propositions, but that they cannot with any show of justice be represented as hypotheses, which are used to predict the course of our sensations; and, accordingly, that the existence of ethics and aesthetics as branches of speculative knowledge presents an insuperable objection to our radical empiricist thesis.

In face of this objection, it is our business to give an account of "judgements of value" which is both satisfactory in itself and consistent with our general empiricist principles. We shall set ourselves to show that in so far as statements of value are significant, they are ordinary "scientific" statements; and that in so far as they are not scientific, they are not in the literal sense significant, but are simply expressions of emotion which can be neither true nor false. In maintaining this view, we may confine ourselves for the present to the case of ethical statements. What is said about them will be found to apply, mutatis mutandis, to the case of aesthetic statements also.

The ordinary system of ethics, as elaborated in the works of ethical philosophers, is very far from being a homogeneous whole. Not only is it apt to contain pieces of metaphysics, and analyses of non-ethical concepts: its actual ethical contents arc themselves of very different kinds. We may divide them, indeed, into four main classes. There are, first of all, propositions which express definitions of ethical terms, or judgements about the legitimacy or possibility of certain definitions. Secondly, there are propositions describing the phenomena of moral experience, and their causes. Thirdly, there are exhortations to moral virtue. And, lastly, there are actual ethical judgements. It is unfortunately the case that the distinction between these four classes, plain as it is, is commonly ignored by ethical philosophers; with the result that it is often very difficult to tell from their works what it is that they are seeking to discover or prove.

In fact, it is easy to see that only the first of our four classes, namely that which comprises the propositions relating to the definitions of ethical terms, can be said to constitute ethical philosophy. The propositions which describe the phenomena of moral experience, and their causes, must be assigned to the science of psychology, or sociology. The exhortations to moral virtue are not propositions at all, but ejaculations or commands which are designed to provoke the reader to action of a certain sort. Accordingly, they do not belong to any branch of philosophy or science. As for the expressions of ethical judgements, we have not yet determined how they should be classified. But inasmuch as they are certainly neither definitions nor comments upon definitions, nor quotations, we may say decisively that they do not belong to ethical philosophy. A strictly philosophical treatise on ethics should therefore make no ethical pronouncements. But it should, by giving an analysis of ethical terms, show what is the category to which all such pronouncements belong. And this is what we are now about to do.

A question which is often discussed by ethical philosophers is whether it is possible to find definitions which would reduce all ethical terms to one or two fundamental terms. But this question, though it undeniably belongs to ethical philosophy, is not relevant to our present inquiry. We are not now concerned to discover which term, within the sphere of ethical terms, is to be taken as fundamental; whether, for example, "good" can be defined in terms of "right" or "right" in terms of "good," or both in terms of "value." What we are interested in is the possibility of reducing the whole sphere of ethical terms to non-ethical terms. We are inquiring whether statements of ethical value can be translated into statements of empirical fact.

That they can be so translated is the contention of those ethical philosophers who are commonly called subjectivists, and of those who are known as utilitarians. For the utilitarian defines the rightness of actions, and the goodness of ends, in terms of the pleasure, or happiness, or satisfaction, to which they give rise; the subjectivist, in terms of the feelings of approval which a certain person, or group of people, has towards them. Each of these types of definition makes moral judgements into a sub-class of psychological or sociological judgements; and for this reason they are very attractive to us. For, if either was correct, it would follow that ethical assertions were not generically different from the factual assertions which are ordinarily contrasted with them; and the account which we have already given of empirical hypotheses would apply to them also.

Nevertheless we shall not adopt either a subjectivist or a utilitarian analysis of ethical terms. We reject the subjectivist view that to call an action right, or a thing good, is to say that it is generally approved of, because it is not self-contradictory to assert that some actions which are generally approved of are not right, or that some things which are generally approved of are not good. And we reject the alternative subjectivist view that a man who asserts that a certain action is right, or that a certain thing is good, is saying that he himself approves of it, on the ground that a man who confessed that he sometimes approved of what was bad or wrong would not be contradicting himself. And a similar argument is fatal to utilitarianism. We cannot agree that to call an action right is to say that of all the actions possible in the circumstances it would cause, or be likely to cause, the greatest happiness, or the greatest balance of pleasure over pain, or the greatest balance of satisfied over unsatisfied desire, because we find that it is not self-contradictory to say that it is sometimes wrong to perform the action which would actually or probably cause the greatest happiness, or the greatest balance of pleasure over pain, or of satisfied over unsatisfied desire. And since it is not self-contradictory to say that some pleasant things are not good, or that some bad things are desired, it cannot be the case that the sentence "x is good" is equivalent to "x is pleasant," or to "x is desired." And to every other variant of utilitarianism with which I am acquainted the same objection can be made. And therefore we should, I think, conclude that the validity of ethical judgements is not determined by the felicific tendencies of actions, any more than by the nature of people's feelings; but that it must be regarded as "absolute" or "intrinsic," and not empirically calculable.

If we say this, we are not, of course, denying that it is possible to invent a language in which all ethical symbols are definable in non-ethical terms, or even that it is desirable to invent such a language and adopt it in place of our own; what we are denying is that the suggested reduction of ethical to non-ethical statements is consistent with the conventions of our actual language. That is, we reject utilitarianism and subjectivism, not as proposals to replace our existing ethical notions by new ones, but as analyses of our existing ethical notions. Our contention is simply that in our language, sentences which contain normative ethical symbols are not equivalent to sentences which express psychological propositions, or indeed empirical propositions of any kind.

It is advisable here to make it plain that it is only normative ethical symbols, and not descriptive ethical symbols, that are held by us to be indefinable in factual terms. There is a danger of confusing these two types of symbols, because they are commonly constituted by signs of the same sensible form. Thus a complex sign of the form "x is wrong" may constitute a sentence which expresses a moral judgement concerning a certain type of conduct, or it may constitute a sentence which states that a certain type of conduct is repugnant to the moral sense of a particular society. In the latter case, the symbol "wrong" is a descriptive ethical symbol, and the sentence in which it occurs expresses an ordinary sociological proposition; in the former case, the symbol "wrong" is a normative ethical symbol, and the sentence in which it occurs does not, we maintain, express an empirical proposition at all. It is only with normative ethics that we are at present concerned; so that whenever ethical symbols are used in the course of this argument without qualification, they are always to be interpreted as symbols of the normative type.

In admitting that normative ethical concepts are irreducible to empirical concepts, we seem to be leaving the way clear for the "absolutist" view of ethics—that is, the view that statements of value are not controlled by observation, as ordinary empirical propositions are, but only by a mysterious "intellectual intuition." A feature of this theory, which is seldom recognized by its advocates, is that it makes statements of value unverifiable. For it is notorious that what seems intuitively certain to one person may seem doubtful, or even false, to another. So that unless it is possible to provide some criterion by which one may decide between conflicting intuitions, a mere appeal to intuition is worthless as a test of a proposition's validity. But in the case of moral judgements no such criterion can be given. Some moralists claim to settle the matter by. saying that they "know" that their own moral judgements are correct. But such an assertion is of purely psychological interest, and has not the slightest tendency to prove the validity of any moral judgement. For dissentient moralists may equally well "know" that their ethical views are correct. And, as far as subjective certainty goes, there will be nothing to choose between them. When such differences of opinion arise in connexion with an ordinary empirical proposition, one may attempt to resolve them by referring to, or actually carrying out, some relevant empirical test. But with regard to ethical statements, there is, on the "absolutist" or "intuitionist" theory, no relevant empirical test. We are therefore justified in saying that on this theory ethical statements are held to be unverifiable. They are, of course, also held to be genuine synthetic proportions.

Considering the use which we have made of the principle that a synthetic proposition is significant only if it is empirically verifiable, it is clear that the acceptance of an "absolutist" theory of ethics would undermine the whole of our main argument. And as we have already rejected the "naturalistic" theories which are commonly supposed to provide the only alternative to "absolutism" in ethics, we seem to have reached a difficult position. We shall meet the difficulty by showing that the correct treatment of ethical statements is afforded by a third theory, which is wholly compatible with our radical empiricism.

We begin by admitting that the fundamental ethical concepts are unanalysable, inasmuch as there is no criterion by which one can test the validity of the judgements in which they occur. So far we are in agreement with the absolutists. But, unlike the absolutists, we are able to give an explanation of this fact about ethical concepts. We say that the reason why they are unanalysable is that they are mere pseudo-concepts. The presence of an ethical symbol in a proposition adds nothing to its factual content. Thus if I say to someone, "You acted wrongly in stealing that money," I am not stating anything more than if I had simply said, "You stole that money." In adding that this action is wrong I am not making any further statement about it. I am simply evincing my moral disapproval of it. It is as if I had said, "You stole that money," in a peculiar tone of horror, or written it with the addition of some special exclamation marks. The tone, or the exclamation marks, adds nothing to the literal meaning of the sentence. It merely serves to show that the expression of it is attended by certain feelings in the speaker.

If now I generalize my previous statement and say, "Stealing money is wrong," I produce a sentence which has no factual meaning—that is, expresses no proposition which can be either true or false. It is as if I had written "Stealing money!!"—where the shape and thickness of the exclamation marks show, by a suitable convention, that a special sort of moral disapproval is the feeling which is being expressed. It is clear that there is nothing said here which can be true or false. Another man may disagree with me about the wrongness of stealing, in the sense that he may not have the same feelings about stealing as I have, and he may quarrel with me on account of my moral sentiments. But he cannot, strictly speaking, contradict me. For in saying that a certain type of action is right or wrong, I am not making any factual statement, not even a statement about my own state of mind. I am merely expressing certain moral sentiments. And the man who is ostensibly contradicting me is merely expressing his moral sentiments. So that there is plainly no sense in asking which of us is in the right. For neither of us is asserting a genuine proposition.

What we have just been saying about the symbol "wrong" applies to all normative ethical symbols. Sometimes they occur in sentences which record ordinary empirical facts besides expressing ethical feeling about those facts: sometimes they occur an sentences which simply express ethical feeling about a certain type of action, or situation, without making any statement of fact. But in every case in which one would commonly be said to be making an ethical judgement, the function of the relevant ethical word is purely "emotive." It is used to express feeling about certain objects, but not to make any assertion about them.

It is worth mentioning that ethical terms do not serve only to express feeling. They are calculated also to arouse feeling, and so to stimulate action. Indeed some of them are used in such a way as to give the sentences in which they occur the effect of commands. Thus the sentence "It is your duty to tell the truth" may be regarded both as the expression of a certain sort of ethical feeling about truthfulness and as the expression of the command "Tell the truth." The sentence "You ought to tell the truth" also involves the command "Tell the truth," but here the tone of the command is less emphatic. In the sentence "It is good to tell the truth" the command has become little more than a suggestion. And thus the "meaning" of the word "good," in its ethical usage, is differentiated from that of the word "duty" or the word "ought." In fact we may define the meaning of the various ethical words in terms both of the different feelings they are ordinarily taken to express, and also the different responses which they are calculated to provoke.

We can now see why it is impossible to find a criterion for determining the validity of ethical judgements. It is not because they have an "absolute" validity which is mysteriously independent of ordinary sense-experience, but because they have no objective validity whatsoever. If a sentence makes no statement at all, there is obviously no sense in asking whether what it says is true or false. And we have seen, that sentences which simply express moral judgements do not say anything. They are pure expressions of feeling and as such do not come under the category of truth and falsehood. They are unverifiable for the same reason as a cry of pain or a word of command is unverifiable—because they do not express genuine propositions.